FARMERS, CRAFTSMEN AND MUSIC MAKERS

LIFE IN A WORCESTERSHIRE VILLAGE BETWEEN THE WARS

FARMERS, CRAFTSMEN AND MUSIC MAKERS

LIFE IN A WORCESTERSHIRE VILLAGE BETWEEN THE WARS

FRED ARCHER

Foreword by PHIL DRABBLE

ALAN SUTTON PUBLISHING LIMITED

First published in the United Kingdom in 1994
Alan Sutton Publishing Limited
Phoenix Mill · Far Thrupp · Stroud · Gloucestershire

First published in the United States of America in 1994
Alan Sutton Publishing Inc. · 83 Washington Street · Dover · NH 03820

British Library Cataloguing in Publication Data

A catalogue record for this book is available from the British Library.

ISBN 0-7509-0572-5

Library of Congress Cataloging in Publication Data applied for

The extract from 'The Watching Post' on p. 157 is reproduced by kind permission
of Sinclair Stevenson Ltd.

Typeset in 11/13 Bembo.
Typesetting and origination by
Alan Sutton Publishing Limited.
Printed in Great Britain by
Butler and Tanner, Frome, Somerset.

To Elsie,

my wife.

For her invaluable

help with the script.

CONTENTS

FOREWORD

Farmers, Craftsmen and Music Makers is vintage Archer at his best. He paints a vivid picture of country life before big business degraded farming from a dignified profession to a mercenary trade, where nothing counts but the bottom line of the balance sheet.

Fred farmed, not for profit but for pride, regarding it as a privilege to leave a better rural heritage for future generations than he found.

He recounts, from practical experience, how he and his forebears tilled their land, instead of expounding theories regurgitated by desk-bound boffins who never soil their hands.

His father farmed 500 acres until the beginning of the First World War. When he died, the farm was split up, Fred's share being 150 acres under Bredon Hill. This was an area made famous by the novelist John Moore, who introduced me to Fred when I was presenting country programmes on steam radio.

They both took part and Fred, who had grown up on the family farm, told me his father had sent him away to school 'to learn to speak proper' because he had picked up the ancient, almost incomprehensible dialect still used by the local farm labourers.

The gaffer at his grammar school was unimpressed, telling him he would have to farm with his feet as he had no brains.

It is obvious from his book that it was Fred who had the higher IQ, and his writing is full of the old Archer magic, making me proud that I can number myself among his friends.

In times of war and slump and national insecurity, there is an instinctive deep nostalgia for the continuity and craftsmanship and seclusion of better days which may have been physically hard but were far more satisfying.

Those who read Fred's book will share the best of rural life as it should be lived.

Phil Drabble
May 1994

INTRODUCTION

Farmers, Craftsmen and Music Makers is a record of some of the folk who lived in the Bredon Hill villages; men and women who were a cut above the ordinary tillers of the soil. Set during the early part of this century, it paints a literary picture of life during the age of the horse, before the countryside was polluted by petrol fumes and chemicals.

The few people who came to the villages from the towns accepted life more or less as it was. Farmers, market gardeners and farm workers caused little in the way of pollution and conservation did exist, although it was not called that then. The smell of the cottagers' pigsty was accepted as a part of country life by the folk who came to live here. The contrast, in summer, of the scent of a field of hay or horse beans was compensation in a way. And no one complained of the early morning cock crow or the mooing of a newly-calved cow missing her calf.

The episodes documented here tell of a time when society was governed by class. But this didn't grate, didn't offend. I know that lots of the characters depicted knew more about life than I did. It was considered good to look above oneself and respect ones 'betters', for in many ways that's what they were. Their presence gave a sense of security and belonging to a close-knit community, making a person strive harder to attain something of the character of these special people.

This book is also about real people, who created a country spirit hard to describe. No one made rules but as it said on the wall of Fred Cormell's barn, 'A Place for Everything, and Everything in its

Place'. Village life was like an orchestra with folk as the instruments, some more powerful than others but all accepted.

Who can but admire the skill and expertise of Fred Cormell, a man of little education but a superb farmer. And what of James Cotton? One of nature's gentlemen, he 'never rubbed his back against a college wall'. His classroom was in the fields, where he could turn his hand to almost anything.

George Hughes, the artist, blended well into village life from Liverpool. As chairman of the parish council, he was looked up to by many and his pictures, painted of scenes in the vale, revealed much of his character. Tiddly Brice, the eccentric who smoked rose petals and hated women, also showed artistic flair and produced some oil paintings *par excellence*.

Hugh Clements was a man of many skills – baker, farmer, football organizer, entertainer, dairyman, church warden. Above all, however, he had what can best be described as 'humanity'. Yes, he cried when he lost his ferret, and sang 'Tomorrow the sun may be shining although it is cloudy today'.

Music from the Cotton family in the 1920s meant a lot to the village as the wireless was not yet a widespread commodity. Ruth, the daughter of James, was to my mind the professional musician. She could make the chapel organ talk and her skill with the piano accordion gave a zest to the concerts of that time. Sunday nights around the piano at the Cottons were special, with James singing the bass and Ralph as tenor.

Laughing Tom, the cow doctor, could cure most animal ailments. A drench of fat bacon and boiled cabbage water usually put right a cow that had lost its cud. He was a pig killer who could keep his bacon sweet even after a year, and who called the flitches his pictures. Why was he called Laughing Tom? He always looked on the bright side.

Under Bredon Hill talented men and women, writers, dramatists and the occasional shepherd, practised country life at its best. This little cell of learning came to Grafton hamlet, nestled beneath

Bredon, below the badger setts of the Firs, and it is a privilege to record such people and events.

Walter, or Bumper, Green had many a tale to tell. Cricketer, pig farmer, rabbit trapper and soldier of the 1914 war, he was the 'Uncle Silas' character of Pigeon Lane.

Percy Attwood, a fine farmer, could be described as a man who fertilized his fields with his feet. I can picture him now, striding across Bredon Hill carrying a tool we called a paddle, spudding the odd thistle on his journey around his cattle, English cattle, Herefords bought at Bridgnorth. Percy was a great cricketer who attained County standard, and I had the privilege of knowing him as a friend.

On the cold side of Bredon the Revers farmed the heavy clay. It was a productive land, but only their experience told them when to work it. They were a family of sportsmen who enjoyed life as it was in the 1920s, with Marjorie rearing turkeys and running the family home, and Mary, now ninety, playing the organ in three churches on Sundays.

Across the fields at Bengrove, the Hopkins family have a small farm. Here we find a continuity that is quite rare today as Paul Hopkins plays wicket-keeper for the Dumbleton team, following a line of Hopkins wicket-keepers begun by his great-grandfather, Teddy Hopkins. I take heart when village young men keep up traditions like these.

Stories of the royal dukes who came to Evesham were told to me by my father and mother, who both worked for a time indirectly for the Orléans family. And while the tales of Lady Norah and The Poor Law give an idea of 1920s Britain, the adventures of William Sexty of Bangrove are surely a direct link with the early Victorians. A good mix of Methodism, hunting, shooting and fishing, these stories depict a life-style one could envy even today.

This book is a social history. I hope you enjoy it. I enjoyed writing it.

CHAPTER ONE

A MUSICAL INTERLUDE

Before the wireless became commonplace it might be thought that music in the village was limited. It was there in church and chapel, and perhaps a few folk had a phonograph or gramophone. But music played a larger part in village life than is instantly apparent. Local folk sang and played instruments at concerts. Folk songs were a part of the scene at the inn. The ploughman whistled and sang as he walked behind his team of horses and the cowman sat under his plum tree playing Sankey hymns on his melodeon on sunny summer evenings.

We read of village orchestras in the writings of Thomas Hardy but in our village they existed well into the 1920s and 1930s. They were all to do with the Cotton family, a village family which goes back hundreds of years, a family steeped in music.

Benjamin Cotton was Parish Clerk until his death in 1879 at the age of ninety-three. James, who could remember the musicians in the gallery of the church before the organ was installed, became head of this remarkable musical family and the Cotton orchestra.

James had a hard upbringing, leaving school as a child unable to read or write. But music was in his blood, a gift inherited from his father. His father played the violin and James told me many times that he spent too much time playing at the village inn. 'He hung his fiddle up at the door,' James said, 'and we were neglected. Never hang your fiddle up at the door.'

As a young man in the 1890s, James became what is known as a believer. He and many more, including my father, became Christians when Mr Knobs, an evangelist, came to the village. To

1

hold his meetings Mr Knobs needed a field to erect his tent and he considered The Close orchard, opposite Holloway Farm where John Baldwyn lived. John was a devout Church of England member and Church Warden at St Barbara's church. At that time there was no Nonconformist chapel in the village and John Baldwyn didn't want one, although there was a group of folk who did.

Fred Cormell, another villager, gave Mr Knobs permission to erect his tent in The Close orchard but on condition that he put it near the road opposite John Baldwyn's sitting-room window. Now Fred Cormell and John Baldwyn were, as our cowman used to say, 'not exactly first cousins'. They were two farmers who never got on together. Fred had been a bailiff before he came to Higford House and the 250 acre farm. He changed the name to The Manor Farm, which annoyed the Baldwyns, who were lords of the manor at Old Manor Farm, at the time, and had been in the village since the thirteenth century.

When Fred gave the evangelist permission to use his field, the village folk were puzzled. 'What's happened to Fred Cormell becoming religious all at once? He's a changed man.' But he wasn't! Fred always said that he carried a stone in his pocket a long time before he threw it. Now he was throwing that stone at John Baldwyn. He knew that the hymn singing and music from Mr Knobs' harmonium would upset him!

Some while afterwards the converts from Mr Knobs' mission built a chapel but not in Fred Cormell's orchard. I don't think Fred would have liked a permanent mission there.

Apart from his music, James Cotton was a bee keeper, a hedge-layer, a water-diviner and a grafter of fruit trees. When he married, his wife taught him to read and soon he became a student of the Bible. Reading music came quite naturally to him, and his sons, Jim and Ralph, were musically gifted too. It was in the little reading room that a Miss Milward taught them to play violas. Miss Milward came with her father and mother to the village from Redditch.

James Cotton, hedge-laying

Mr Milward had a factory there making needles, pins and fish hooks.

This then was the beginning of the Cotton Orchestra. When in full swing the group of village musicians consisted of: James on the big bass viol, Jim on the viola, Ralph on the viola, and Ruth on the cello. Later on Ruth played the piano accordion and was very proficient on both organ and piano.

That Cotton Orchestra, playing at concerts and in the chapel in the 1920s, is an image which remains today. A group of village folk making music, James in his dark Sunday suit and his white shirt fronts, Jim and Ralph in neat lounge suits, with Ralph wearing spats over brown shoes.

These three bowler-hatted men were a part of those Sundays as they walked to the village chapel. Ralph was the more flamboyant character, his viola swung with him as he played. A lot of feeling went from his bow to the strings, and he could carry the congregation with him. When he played the chorus of a Sankey hymn he would repeat the chorus after the last verse, and the congregation would follow.

Ralph was a man of great character, certainly not a 'yes man' or one who made compromises. He did have a unique sense of humour though. Meeting him on a summer's day, you would call out, 'A nice day, Ralph', and he would reply, 'A good day to change a pound note.'

Ralph, like his father, was an expert with fruit trees and he was also an early motor cyclist. But music to him was life at its best. He had a very mellow tenor voice which complimented James' bass.

Village concerts in the old army hut, a relic of the First World War, were popular when the Cotton players, with Ruth playing the piano, accompanied the singing. William Sanford, a market gardener, had what was said to be a good tenor voice. He brought with him a tuning fork which he struck before he performed.

'Do, Do, Do,' he called, then Ruth played the introduction for his two songs, 'The Campbells are Coming, a ho and a ho' and

Ralph Cotton

'The March of the Cameron Men'. The last, he informed us, was the signature tune of the East Lancs Regiment. As William peered at the music fixed on Ruth's piano the oil lamps flickered a yellow glow. There was only one copy of the score and William's eyesight was not that good.

'You will have to excuse us if mistakes are made,' he said. 'Ruth and I have only one line between us.'

A farmer, a natural comedian, in the audience that evening called out, 'Mr Sanford, what on earth are you and Ruth going to do on washing day if you have only got one line between you?'

The audience laughed, but I don't think William was amused.

John Ellis, a painter and decorator who sang bass in the choir in the church, was back stage clearing up jellies and blancmanges left over from the tea. The concert followed the tea. He plumped a great bale of music on the top of the piano. One ballad after another was played by Ruth and sung by John, until the Master of Ceremonies decided we needed a change.

Ruth played pieces on her accordion. Tunes from the First World War were popular. This particular concert was on Armistice Day and the old soldiers were guests. Tom Barnett, the thatcher, sang with great feeling, 'It's Only a Beautiful Picture in a Beautiful Golden Frame'. There was nothing effeminate about this man; indeed, one could call him a man and a half.

On Boxing Day the bell-ringers sang carols around the village. Their singing was memorable in those pre-wireless days. Under a lantern fixed to a bean pole the local carols, collected by Amy Roberson, meant so much at Christmas: 'Arise you sleepy souls, arise', the 'Withy Carol', and their *pièce de résistance* 'While Shepherds Watched' to the tune 'Lyneham'.

The Beckford handbell ringers

'Be the little 'uns abed?' Ralph, one of the ringers, asked Dad at the door. We were not abed, we wanted to hear the ringers. Frank Whittle, who came on crutches having lost a leg in the First World War, had a voice like Paul Robeson. They performed their final song, finishing it off by singing the last line, 'Begin and nev, begin and nev, begin and never cease.'

Dad gave his contribution to the ringers but said, 'It would be a bad job if you chaps began and never ceased.' All good fun. It was a gem at Christmas.

Ewart Morrison sang at village concerts and took prominent roles in amateur operatics. A favourite song of his was 'Trumpeter, What Are You Sounding Now', with which he charmed the ladies of the village. He was handsome to the extreme, a village man who played cricket for Gloucestershire and lived the life of a gentleman. Immaculately dressed in blue pin-stripes and smoking Sarony cigarettes, this man was a cut above everyone. He drove a Standard car when few folk had cars. I remember him driving slowly down the village with George Hughes, the artist, the leathered elbows of his Harris Tweed jacket resting on the door of the car and kid gloves on his hands. He worked at one time for the Farmers Union Insurance. He served in the 1914 war, and again in 1939, was taken prisoner, escaped, and played a leading role in the film *The Last Chance*. He was a born actor.

Ewart was also a professional singer, his stance beside the piano having the 'Edwardian drawing-room' touch. James Cotton, on the other hand, was a true son of the soil and put on no frills when he sang. But he had a sense of humour born in the fields, telling me that God loved the crow as much as the nightingale.

Some years ago I had the pleasure of taking tea with Mr and Mrs J.B. Priestley at their home near Stratford-upon-Avon. There are two things which impressed me about Mr Priestley, apart from his writing. One was his love of music and the other was his pipe. We sat together in his library smoking our pipes. He was a connoisseur of tobacco but said he would smoke anything. I shared some of my

James Cotton water-divining by the Tibble Stone

quite ordinary brand with him. His knowledge of music amazed me as he sat at the grand piano and made a comment I'll never forget. He said every time a violin is taken up to the lumber room, or a piano carted away, and a gadget put in their place that turns music on and off like tap water we move another step away from sanity and take to snarling harder than ever.

Opening a fête that year where one of the items on the programme was a piano-smashing competition I appreciated his sentiments as sledge-hammer blows rained down on the ivories of a one-time precious musical instrument.

Down at the parish church of St Barbara, Bunch Baldwyn played the organ. The resonance from that instrument when she played 'The Dead March from Saul' at funerals was unbelievable. The whole structure of the church vibrated, giving a moving tribute to the deceased.

Bunch was a single lady, one of a family who had been a part of the village for five hundred years. The last of the Baldwyns to live in Ashton died last year. She was Mary Roberson, the daughter of the doctor who married Amy Baldwyn. It was Amy who collected the carols which had been sung at Christmas for centuries.

Bunch lived in constant fear of thunder and lightning and was often in conflict with Harold Wigley, who kept the churchyard neat and tidy. He borrowed her bass broom and wore it out.

'Harold, there's not many bristles left on my broom. You have made the path up the churchyard wide enough for a bus, you stupid man,' she told him. Harold sniffed, puffed his pipe and walked away.

There was a love–hate relationship between this pair. Harold was well mannered, a polite man. One winter evening he was walking the path from the churchyard to the village street past Bunch's garden. Bunch had several stone figures in her garden and one life-sized one stood by the path Harold was taking. Bunch was at her back door some yards away. In the twilight, Harold thought the

Ralph Cotton and his mother

figure was Bunch, and he raised his hat to it saying, 'Good night, Bunch.'

Although the figure was a flattering image of Miss Bunch Baldwyn, she had the final say. Many of her ancestors were buried in the family vault in the churchyard. Bunch was proud of them and constantly reminded Harold that she had more bones in the churchyard than he had.

In the 1920s music in the village was still very much a reminder of life some fifty years earlier. Ralph, our carter, sang behind the plough as I drove the team. He walked with a nautical roll singing:

> I love the green fields,
> I love the sun shine,
> The robin with pretty red breast.
> I love pussy cat fast asleep on the mat.
> I love my own Mother the best.

Cecil Sharp, that great collector of folk songs, said that at the turn of the century England was a 'nest of singing birds' in every country village. He said that those he spoke to, the old folk in particular, told him that everyone sang on their way to work, at work, and while returning home in the evening.

I wonder, perhaps, if Cecil Sharp's view was a little exaggerated. Maybe, but labourers and their women folk did sing as they worked as well as in church or chapel.

One man who must not be ignored was a plasterer named Leonard, who turned his hand to some intricate work. Len made gravestones from granite chippings for poor folk who couldn't afford the stonemason. He had a very keen ear for music, was quite good with a mouth-organ, had a good tenor voice in chapel, but was a wizard on what he called 'the ivories'. He would hear a tune only once and then be able to repeat it perfectly. He used to refer to himself as another Charlie Kunz.

Classical music didn't worry him. He would play pieces from Handel as well as the popular tunes of the day. Lubrication with cider in the local pub did help his playing. One evening, playing 'Jesu Joy of Man's Desiring', Leonard didn't know how to finish. But then it's that sort of tune.

For hundreds of years England had produced men and women with a song in their hearts; their own music made with the most primitive and most beautiful of instruments – the human voice. A song would be handed down from father to son, mother to daughter, and in the process would become shaped by its owner for his or her purpose. Every time it was sung it gained a little and it altered a little and it was never sung twice the same way.

One winter night in 1923 a wireless concert was arranged to take place in the army hut. Sam Grove had a music shop in Evesham selling at that time gramophones and records, and then he got involved in the wireless. Sam came over that morning with his wireless set and equipment. An aerial was erected from Mr Nicklin's walnut tree to our barn, complete with insulators. A bucket was buried in the ground for an earth wire to be connected.

At six o'clock the army hut, known as the Recreation Room, was full of villagers. From London, Big Ben struck in our village for the first time. The varied programme was enjoyed by one and all, although some were rather sceptical. Shepherd Tidmarsh was dubious that the striking of Big Ben came from London, as he said, 'To hear Beckford church clock strike two miles away the wind had to be in the right direction.'

After the concert Percy Wigley, Harold's brother, a retired engineer from Birmingham, started making wireless sets in the village. Percy, a bit of a whiz-kid, ran a Douglas motor bike on paraffin when petrol was short. He made sets and sold them. Ernest Roberts, who kept a garage at Beckford, was soon making three-valve sets and charging the batteries of the listeners-in.

When a party came to the old army hut in 1927 and performed extracts from *Messiah* it was a far cry from the Huddersfield Choral Society, but they tried. By then, though, lots of the villagers had a wireless set and it was hard to compete.

Here then was a revolution in village life. No longer were we dependent on local music, no longer dependent on Beech's hooter from the jam factory for telling us the time, but we were members of a much wider world brought to us on the wireless. We got the news without buying a paper, heard Bransbury Williams as Scrooge at Christmas and could listen to fine singers and full orchestras. The change had come to our lives.

CHAPTER TWO

PERCY ATTWOOD, GENTLEMAN FARMER

Percy Attwood can rightly be described as a gentleman farmer. He was both a farmer and a gentleman. He was not the sort of chap who rode around his acres just giving orders to his men; he took his jacket off at haymaking and harvest, pitching and loading from morning until night.

Percy's father owned The Close, an Elizabethan house at Ashton under Hill, and the farm around it, although when I knew them the family were living at Conderton, four miles away. I used to see Percy when I was a boy striding across Bredon Hill from The Laurels at Conderton to his land at Ashton under Hill. Latterly I farmed the land which had been in his family since the enclosures of 1783.

Percy was a useful cricketer in his young days, playing for Malvern College and with the Foster brothers, who played for Worcestershire. In those days Worcestershire Cricket Club was known as Fostershire because there were so many Fosters in the team. Percy used to speak of that character Clockey Arnold, who was so drunk at one match on the county ground that the captain, Foster, said, 'Here we are playing Yorkshire and we have only sixty on the board with six wickets down and Arnold is drunk.'

Arnold replied, 'I'll bet you a sovereign that I'll make fifty.' He staggered to the wicket and saw the ball as big as a football and flogged the fours around the ground. 'Mind you,' Percy told me, 'I wouldn't recommend batting when drunk.'

Percy Attwood, born in 1874, was a typical Victorian. His roots were in the soil, farming land in three parishes. I visited him regularly in his retirement when he was content to grow fruit, vegetables and flowers in his garden.

One evening by the fireside his mind went back to the time he studied music in Evesham. His brother became a distinguished scholar of music but Percy was destined for farming. As we both looked into the fire Percy said wryly, 'Have you ever ridden a pony on a dark night?'

I admitted that that was a thing I'd never experienced.

He went on, 'As a boy I used to ride my pony to Evesham and back, which was about fifteen miles, for music lessons.' His face lit up as he relived the scene. 'Do you know that wide grass verge by Hinton Turn?'

I told him I knew it well. It was where we let the cattle graze as we had our bait on the way to Evesham market.

'There is a grip there to take the surface water off the road and I was cantering along the grass verge one dark night on my way home from music lessons and my pony jumped high in the air just to clear the grip. He saw the trench but, of course, I didn't.' I nodded, interested, picturing the scene as the twelve-year-old boy in breeches rode his pony home along a car-free main road. Then Percy added, 'It was a strange sensation jumping high in the dark.'

These recollections were in 1966 when my friend was ninety-two, but he clearly recalled Joseph Arch, the early pioneer of the Agricultural Union, speaking to the men on the land from a farm wagon in the evening. Percy said that he used to have tea with Miss Sparks who kept a Dames School in the village.

'You actually saw Joseph Arch then?' I asked.

'Many times, but my men didn't need the Union then. I paid over the rate and they had plenty of cider, free milk, firewood and they grew their potatoes on headlands in the fields.'

Noticing that Percy had no television set and mentioning the fact, for I knew that cricket to him was a religion, he told me his

Percy Attwood, gentleman farmer

eyesight was not good so he listened to the test matches on radio. We talked of cricket; he remembered W.G. Grace and a fellow who farmed under Bredon Hill who had bowled Grace out at a charity match. Percy told me, 'That umpire from Ashton under Hill, the ladder maker, said "Not out" when the farmer bowled Grace out. Then he said, "We biunt come yer to see thee bowl, we be come yer to see Grace bat."'

'You kept wicket, I gather, for Overbury,' I said.

'Yes, and was captain for many years,' he replied.

When I asked him of memorable matches he played in he replied after some thought, 'One against the Cheltenham Police in 1921. It was a very hot summer and the wicket was as hard as the Turn Pike Road and we had a fast bowler, Walter Green, known as Bumper Green. He was inclined to bowl short. The second ball Walter bowled from the first over may have dropped on a plantain, it hit a police sergeant under the jaw and he dropped down like a stone. They carried him off. A young constable came in next and Walter's next ball skimmed his temples as he ducked. I called to Walter from behind the wicket, "Send the rest of the over down steady and that will do for today before someone gets killed."'

Mentioning Lindwall as a fast bowler Percy remembered some of the greats in the Australian team. 'I've been to Australia twice, quite an experience in 1903. Mother went with me and she kept her shoes on all night in case the ship sank.'

I asked this veteran farmer about the parties in the farm houses in the old days.

'Oh, yes. We had real parties in those days,' he replied. 'We arrived at farm houses around the hill about 6.30 on winter nights. You know, the candle lamps and the oil lamps on our spring carts and traps were a far cry from the lights on modern motor cars!' Percy smiled as he recalled the winter scene in the Bredon Hill villages. He then told me how parties were arranged when the moon was full and that almanacs were very explicit, noting the changes of the moon.

'What did you do at the parties?' I asked the veteran bachelor, wondering why no lady had captured his heart.

'Oh, we danced to the music of piano and violin, played cards and drank port. Mind you, Christmas parties went on for a fortnight and often finished in the small hours. Where your brother farms there's a nag stable, groom's bothy and trap house, the upstairs was called the Ballroom. That's where some of the best dances took place. The Wesson family lived in the house at Old Manor Farm. Percy Nind courted Miss Wesson but he was a bit forward, you know.'

Knowing Percy Nind, I wondered how forward he had been and asked Mr Attwood what he meant.

'Well, I won't go into the details but farming men on the whole treated the ladies with respect. Miss Wesson was having none of Master Nind's nonsense and gave him a big smack across his mouth and told him to leave. Tustin Vale, the carter for Mr Roberts, looked after the horses in the nag stable. He saddled Master Nind's horse. Nothing came of the relationship. You know Tustin Vale was a bit thick. One winter's night I looked at him in the nag stable and said, "Whatever have you done to your hair?" "Oh," he replied, "the Missus started to cut it at tea time and hadn't time to finish it. Her's gwain to finish it tomorrow night." That was Tustin all over.'

'Mr Attwood,' I continued that evening, 'I've seen that picture of you smoking a pipe. Do you still smoke?'

'No, not now, gave it up years ago, but I always smoked at parties.'

When I suggested cigars he replied, 'My goodness no! You see we used long churchwarden pipes and had our names written on them in pencil. Then at the end of the party the pipes were all put in a wicker basket and kept until the next time we met. Every farmer had his basket of pipes.

At ninety-two Percy Attwood was giving me an insight into village life in Edwardian England, when there was no need to call farming 'organic' as that's what it always was. All the land was cropped in rotation and farmyard manure applied in quantity. The corn crops were not so heavy it is true, and new varieties of wheat and barley yield enormous crops – but at what price?

Percy said that he was a great believer in fattening cattle in the fields with the help of linseed and cotton cake and that the dung from these cattle improved the grass land enormously. 'It's a better way than using chemicals,' he said. 'The cow-pats when spread by the chain harrow enrich the ground, but sometimes when the dung is set I used to employ women with small shuppicks [pitchforks] to turn the pats over but that wasn't always necessary. The badgers were good allies at night. They would turn the cow-pats over looking for grubs and beetles.'

He then told me how he rented a field on Bredon Hill with poor pasture and his landlord paid for a truck load of cattle cake to be sent to Beckford station for Percy to feed the cattle so that the dung would enrich the ground. We spoke of field names and their meanings on the farm I farmed after him: Holbrook, a field near the brook where the holly grows (holly was used to make the short stick on threshing flails); Catbrain, a field which was a mixture of clay and gravel, a Kentish word; Van Deeman's Land, a relic of transportation days no doubt.

When I told Percy that I had to plough quite a lot of the pasture up during the war he seemed hurt. His was a generation who believed it took years to create a good pasture. He may have been right.

'By Holbrook was a good feeding pasture,' Percy's voice had a solemn ring to it when he said these words. He continued, 'I used to buy store cattle from Bridgnorth before the 1914 war at £15 each, run them in Big Holbrook for the summer and sell them at £22 each. Thomas Barnett looked after them well. He and my other men worked for me all their lives and when they retired I doubled their old age pension.'

Not long after this visit to Mr Attwood he fell and broke his femur and died shortly afterwards. Had he not had this accident he may have made another century, like he did several times on the cricket field.

CHAPTER THREE

OLD SOLDIERS – THEY SHALL GROW NOT OLD

These words of Laurence Binyon were written when the First World War was fresh in people's minds. Most of the men who served their country then are no longer with us but we remember them still.

Jack Cook, a Victorian who lived under the shadow of Bredon Hill at Wyre Piddle, saw service in the Middle East during the First World War. His father was crippled with arthritis and unable to work, which made it necessary for Jack to leave school at thirteen. He worked on a market garden. His first job, he said with a smile, was turning the grindstone for the cabbage cutters to sharpen their knives. He then learned the art of packing cabbages in the withy-made hampers. In April he learnt how to prune fruit trees and puddled the blue clay for the men who did the grafting. Mr Gardner, his boss, was a very particular man, never using horses among the fruit trees. All the ground was dug by men every winter.

The boss, Jack told me, had seven daughters, all fine, pretty girls. The village boys were given jobs to do on Saturday mornings and of course these seven girls were a draw. You know what they say – the two most powerful things in this world are gunpowder, that'll blow you up, and women, that'll draw you.

'How many boys do you think I have seen around the farm on Saturday mornings?' Jack asked me. I didn't hazard a guess. 'Believe me,' he replied, 'forty, and they would do all the odd jobs around the farm.'

I smiled and thought the odds were long.

In those days when the market gardens were dressed with farmyard manure he told me of picking 63 pounds of gooseberries off one bush and 46 pots, each of 56 pounds, of Newton Wonder apples off one tree.

Christmas 1907 found Jack, only a boy, picking sprouts with the men. The weather was bitterly cold so the boss sent a jar of plum jerkum (plum wine) to encourage them at their work and hopefully keep out the cold. Forty pots of sprouts and forty pots of sprout tops were stacked on the headland. The foreman fetched another jar of plum jerkum and one by one the men lay under the hedge leaving young thirteen-year-old Jack to load the dray himself and drive it to Pershore station.

A very violent thunderstorm struck the Vale of Evesham one summer when Jack was a boy. One of his recollections concerned a tragedy on a neighbouring farm. The farm's carter was ploughing with a three horse team in line when lightning struck the hames of the harness on the foremost horse and passed along the traces and killed the whole team in the furrow. The ploughman fortunately survived.

Jack drove what he called the awkward squad, a team of three horses at plough. The filler was an Irish nag, in front a fourteen hands cob, while the foremost was a cream coloured army horse named Noble, who had served in the Boer War. Noble had been used in South Africa in a gun carriage team and never forgot his experiences on the battlefield.

'One Saturday morning we boys, two of us, thought of a game we could play with the carter on the farm. (This was a couple of years before I left school.) The carter was harrowing the ground ready for pea planting in March with Noble, the old war horse. We watched from behind the hedge waiting for the carter to turn on the headland then shouted "Charge". Noble ran full gallop across the field.'

Plough-boys did have a hard time in those far-off days. They got the blame for things that went wrong on the land and some carters were quite cruel to them. I suppose they can be excused for taking it out on the older men on occasions.

Jack Cook, though, was really too busy for pranks, for he had a disabled father. Although the village butcher sent a joint of meat as a gift every Saturday, times were hard. Jack used to fish on the River Avon after dark and he recalls catching twelve 6 pound chub during one night.

Just before his call up in 1914 Jack learned to drive a lorry. He said it was a Striker Squire (I've never heard of such a make). He used it for hauling granite from the Malvern quarries and once saw four generations of stone breakers there, wearing gauze spectacles to protect their eyes as they worked with their hammers. The oldest was eighty and the youngest in his teens.

Jack is one of the many remembered on the village war memorial as one of the men who 'were a wall unto us by night and day'.

As folk pass on to pastures new I always regret that so much of their character, moulded over a lifetime, goes with them, forgotten as a dream. Such is the case with Howard Pritchitt. Howard was a Cotswold man born and bred, but his niece, Gwen Bury, lived under Bredon Hill and so I became acquainted with Howard.

Howard had travelled widely in his younger days and listening to his reminiscences as he sat in his Windsor chair by the fireside was both an education and a privilege. But talking to this gentleman, who was in his seventies, I had to be careful to listen, rather than pass an opinion. He was of a generation before me and he let me know that. However, we did form a friendship.

'When we had a glass of home-made wine,' he would say, 'elderberry, parsnip or plum, then we were gentlemen. Ah, we were gentlemen.' And he certainly was. Howard was a man who had what is known as a presence.

He was one of the real gentlemen of the land, a farmer and threshing contractor who with his family had tilled the land with steam ploughs, horses and simple tackle. As we talked I realized that

Howard was one of the last of the men on the land who had worked like this. As a boy he drove a team of six bullocks at plough. They were expert at their job and never paddled the ground, however wet the stubbles were. When the ploughman stopped for half an hour for his mid-morning snack or bait, as it was called, the bullocks rested by lying down in the furrow to chew their cud, their traces loose.

For many years Howard drove a carrier's cart to market towns in Gloucestershire, Warwickshire and Worcestershire, and his stories of life in Victorian England were legion. He told me how his father, grandfather and great-grandfather were carriers for the last 150 years. I was curious to know what Pritchitt's carrier's carts had carried over those Cotswold hills early in the century.

'Oh, all manner of things,' he replied. 'There were coffins to be taken to Swindon, barrels of beer, and one day, among all the other things, I brought back a glass eye from Warwick for a chap in the village. There was no National Health then. Every day we went to Cirencester taking women shopping, six pence return.'

When I asked him what the shoppers bought, Howard replied in a most forthright manner, 'Something serviceable. Not like today. They bought corduroys for the men, something to last.'

Howard had once carried thirty passengers in one go to the Cirencester Mop. The carrier's cart is now in the Bristol Museum.

Howard had also been a member of an old minstrel troop who entertained with blacked faces in villages and towns. I still remember a few lines of one of his songs:

> All the girls are busy knitting jumpers,
> All day long, all day long.
> Knit one, drop one, one row plain, one row pearl,
> Busy knitting jumpers all day long.

Howard still had a good singing voice in his seventies and his memories of days gone by brought a twinkle to his eye and colour to his cheeks. 'Shall I sing you a song, one I sung fifty years ago?' he asked on one visit. I nodded and he sang 'The Farmer's Boy'.

'You see,' he continued, 'songs today have no meaning. Mind you, we never sang songs about work. We left that behind us.'

Howard once told me of a barber named Harry Fosbrook, who cut his hair with blunt scissors and fetched tears to his eyes. He used to shave his customers with a cutthroat razor. He would dip the instrument in boiling water and sometimes jokingly draw the back of the blade across the throat of the man in the chair.

On another occasion Howard wondered if he had ever told me about 'old John Green'. 'I don't think so,' I said.

'Well, he was ill one Christmas and his wife got me to fetch the doctor from Northleach. I knocked him up at midnight and he came where old John was gasping his last. His wife was piping her eyes at the bedside. The doctor turned to me and said, "Pritchitt, what a fool you have been to fetch me, the man's dead."

'Old John rose up and said, "I biunt dead, Doctor."

'His missus stopped crying but told John to "Shut up. The doctor knows best."

'We kept some good horses on the farm and the carters in those days seemed to think more of their horses than they did of their wives. I caught our carter stealing cattle cake from the granary for the horses. When I told him off he replied, "I don't care if you clouts me and gives me the sack and kicks me, I'll fight back." Such was the concern the man had for his team of horses.'

Howard was fond of his own horses but did away with cruppering their tails and merely used the crupper to hang up the hames. He said they worked more comfortable like that.

Howard joined up at the start of the First World War and was on the Western Front when the Christmas truce was called in the trenches.

' 'Twas like this,' he recalled. 'The Jerries were so close you could hear them talking in their trench. On Christmas Day we all came out of the trenches, got together and shared our rations. We wished each other Merry Christmas and someone in our lot had a football so we played against the Jerries after dinner. One young German soldier, a bit more educated than the rest, spoke English. I said to him as we sat eating our Bully Beef, "It breaks my heart to think I've got to shoot thee tomorrow."

'"Nien, Nien, Tommy, we are friends. No shoot me, me no shoot you."

'I replied, "My orders be to shoot thee in the morning now that Christmas is over."'

Howard told me he had no intentions of shooting the fellow and that he was but a boy and the politicians started the war.

'Looking back to 1914, Howard,' I said, 'don't you think this situation was ridiculous when it all started again on Boxing Day?'

''Course it was,' Howard replied. 'But next morning back in the trenches the young German showed his head above ground. I shouted "Keep thee yud down" across that No Man's Land and I showered some bullets into the sand bags well above the German's head. You can't kill a fella in cold blood, no way.'

After the Second World War Howard's daughter married an American serviceman. He wasn't too keen on the Yanks, so after the wedding he put a cheque for £200 on the table at the reception and said to his daughter, 'Here's your fare home when you are tired of him.'

Howard visited the couple in the States later, travelling out on the *Queen Elizabeth*. But he decided to come home by plane. On the runway Howard spoke to the pilot. 'Bist thee a driving this thing?' he questioned.

'Yes,' was the reply.

'Well mind what thee bist at, 'cos I got to see my sheep on my farm tomorrow.'

Halfway across the Atlantic Howard was uneasy. He went to the flight-deck, saying to the pilot, 'See that black cloud in front, that's a thunderstorm. Bist a going over the top or underneath 'cos now's the time to make your mind up.'

Back with his sheep the next day he told me the story of a man in a local pub, sitting there with a newspaper upside down. Howard said to him, 'You got the paper upside down.'

'Well,' the old chap replied, 'any fool can read the paper the right way up.'

On my last visit to Howard, at the time when men were landing on the moon, he was in a philosophical mood. Just as he didn't hold with modern farming, so he didn't agree with any of the ways the world was going.

'What dost think of this caper of men going to the moon?' he asked. Before I could reply he went on, 'The Almighty put the sun up there for us by day and the moon by night. The Government has made a right mess down here and we have no right to interfere with the moon.'

I smiled and told him the story about a chap in our village who remarked in the pub one night on the failure of one attempt to reach the moon. He said, 'I knew damn well they wouldn't get there. They should have gone last week – it was only just over the hill.'

CHAPTER FOUR

THE ARTISTS OF BREDON HILL

Before the First World War the village population was divided, shall we say, into three classes. There were the farmers and landowners, then the folk who have been described as the Little Master Men (smallholders), including publicans, shopkeepers, blacksmiths and wheelwrights, and station-masters. The third group were the farm workers, railway men and roadmen.

At that time, when travel by rail was popular, people from elsewhere were visiting the village, staying at the pub, and enjoying the way of life in a village in the country. When a cottage became vacant and up for sale these folk competed with the locals at the auction. Who were these visitors from Birmingham, Liverpool and London? Some came here to retire but there were two distinguished artists among the new villagers – George Hughes and Edward (Tiddly) Brice.

George Hughes came from Liverpool. He went to school with F.E. Smith, who became Lord Birkenhead. He started work after his grammar school education as clerk in one of the Liverpool banks. George stuck it for a time but was not happy shut away in an office. The palaver over the annual balance on 1 January one year was the turning point in his career. He told me that the figures that New Year were one shilling and three pence out. The clerks worked hard until after midnight to trace the discrepancy in the figures. George just wanted to go home. He was fed up with the system. Putting his hand into his trouser pocket he said, 'Here, take this one shilling and three pence and let's get off home.'

'We can't do that,' the under-manager replied. 'The balance has to be made, however late we are here.'

George left the bank. He married and bought Orchard Cottage at Ashton under Hill. His hobby as an artist became his full-time profession. Soon his talent was recognized and his paintings hung in the main galleries of the land. Inspired by the scenery of the Vale of Evesham, Bredon Hill and the Cotswolds, George Hughes made a name for himself in the Gloucestershire and Worcestershire countryside.

When I first knew George Hughes he was a mature man. He was chairman of our parish council. Dad was one of the five members. When I started school at five years old and travelled by train to Evesham, Mr Hughes was often on the five past four train on the little branch line to our station. We schoolboys would join him in his carriage. This smart, dapper man in a well-cut tweed suit and grey trilby was so fond of children. He and his wife never had a family but both of them were most generous. Mr Hughes always carried a little leather case with his name suitably engraved, G.H. Hughes. I was always fascinated by his hair style, wavy and golden with a short kiss curl over his brow. I am glad I never knew until I left school that George's hair was a wig. At birthdays and Christmas he and his wife gave books for presents but meeting him on the train was special.

In the waiting-room at our little station on the branch line were two things I remember. First, a weighing machine and second, a penny in the slot machine for Nestlé milk chocolate. When we arrived at our station and went over the level crossing, Mr Hughes would put his hand into his trouser pocket and bring out pennies. 'Now,' he would say, 'how about chocolate. First, all you boys stand there quite still by the machine.'

He would take a penny and put it under my collar. I would feel the coin go down into the top of my grey flannel short trousers and stick there.

'Jump about a bit,' he would call out, and as he laughed the coin would fall on the floor of the waiting-room. Those Nestlé chocolate bars were only thin, but welcome refreshment before we walked the half mile to our house with Mr George Hughes.

George Hughes' hobby was cricket. He was a loyal member of Gloucestershire Cricket Club, who in those days were high up in the County Championship. When our village became a part of Worcestershire Mr Hughes was quite upset. He supported Gloucestershire, and Worcestershire were at the bottom of the league!

George Hughes could be described as a good man. He was not a church-goer, having no time for what he called the Robed Clergy. However, he did support the village Baptist chapel financially. He rarely attended but his cottage stood opposite the chapel and on many Sunday nights George could be seen at his cottage door, listening to the hymn singing.

When the lich-gate was erected down at St Barbara's church Harold Wigley, secretary of the church council, insisted that it was locked, despite the fact there was a footpath through the churchyard to the hamlet of Paris on Bredon Hill. By the side of the lich-gate there was a kissing-gate, but mothers with prams and push-chairs could not get through. The parish council, under George Hughes, ordered Harold and the parson, who was responsible, to unlock the gate. They refused. This did not help George Hughes' attitude towards the Established Church.

When George Hughes died the village lost a distinguished artist and a gentleman. I saw him raise his hat in the street to the woman who did his washing.

Edward Kington Brice was a more distinguished artist than George Hughes it is true. He was not, however, such a gentleman. He came to the village just after the First World War. A bachelor with a big chip on his shoulder, he never really integrated with the rural folk and was always at odds with somebody. He was very suspicious of women, too, was Edward. A friend of mine bought the fruit, plums and apples, in Brice's garden. This was quite a common practice in the 1920s. Bert, my friend, picked the plums from all but one tree, a tall Belle de Louvain. Next to Mr Brice's garden, Mrs X lived in her little cottage. Bert knew that she had a long forty rung ladder. 'I shall have to borrow Mrs X's ladder,' Bert said to Mr Brice.

But Mr Brice replied, 'Don't you dare bring her ladder into my garden. She is the Woman Devil, a terrible character.'

At a meeting held to organize the jubilee sports in 1935 Brice upset the women there too. It had been suggested that every man in the village had a little beer at the sportsfield. Brice said, 'It's not a good idea. Men can't run and jump when full of beer.' The women turned on him saying their husbands were not drunkards.

Saying that though, Brice did have to rely on a woman to do his washing, and her husband told me he was so mean that he rarely changed the bottom sheet on his bed. George said in his usual outspoken style, 'There's a mark down the middle of the sheet, the mark of Brice, just where he lies at night.'

I recall Mr Brice as a smallish man dressed in a pepper and salt suit and fawn trilby. He rode a Sunbeam green bicycle with his easel strapped along the crossbar. On sunny days he could be seen by the moat pond, painting a landscape of the elm trees bordering the water with moorhens swimming among the pond weed, and ewes and lambs grazing the grassy banks. I bought that oil painting off him many years ago. It's a gem. Brice was a professional with letters after his name. Perhaps, unlike James Cotton, he did rub his back against a college wall.

After the picture was purchased Mr Brice asked if he could come down to the farmhouse and see it hung. He arrived one evening in the winter. In our lounge the picture hung over the fireplace and of course the room was lit by electricity.

'Um . . . um,' he grunted. 'What a pity.'

'Anything wrong, Mr Brice?' I said.

'Yes, everything's wrong. This electric light does spoil the look of my picture. Now get an oil lamp instead and with the yellow light it will look good.'

We didn't get an oil lamp, but no doubt he had a point.

I used to visit him frequently after that at his house up Cottons Lane, known by the locals as Bachelors Avenue. Yes, the lane was populated with bachelors. His house, called Bum Bo, had been the farmhouse where Jim Jeynes had his dairy herd. When Mr Brice died someone changed the name of the house to Ye Old Well House. But it's still Bum Bo to me! I never cared for changing names of houses or streets.

The visits to Mr Brice were always an experience for me. He was known as Tiddly Brice and the rhyme in the village went as follows:

> Tiddly Brice bought a pound of rice
> And grumbled at the price.
> Old Tiddly Brice.

When he came to the village after serving in the First World War, he put a new roof on Bum Bo. The roof, very much in keeping with the stone building and mullion windows, was of wooden tiles known as shingles, which mellowed with age. As I entered through the front door I saw a large wooden bowl filled with rose petals on a mahogany table. It gave a pot pourri scent to Bum Bo.

'Lovely,' I remarked. 'The smell of roses.'

'Huh . . . huh!' Mr Brice smiled and grunted again, 'Huh. That's part of my smoking mixture.' He then explained that when the petals were dry he mixed them with strong tobacco for his pipe.

'You can't pay ten pence an ounce for tobacco these days, you have to economize.'

As we sat together in the ingle with Edward's pipe going nicely the smell from the mixture was quite pleasant.

At the bottom of the village near the moat pond a tithe barn stood in an apple orchard. It was quite a small building known as Tythe Court. It had been built on bricks and there was an open shed for carts and wagons. The building on the first floor was approached by wooden steps from the outside. It was here that Mr Brice had his studio. A large window which formed part of the roof looked over the apple orchard on the north side.

I suppose that in the past tithes were paid to the parson of St Barbara's, but when we farmed that land none were paid until Revd Baker searched out some old papers which proved that we had to pay him nine shillings and five pence a year.

Some of Edward Brice's best pictures were of Tythe Court Orchard. One water-colour he did was of a fallen tree, an apple tree in blossom. The trunk of the tree lay horizontal in the orchard while the branches looked up to the sky. Underneath, a ewe and her young lamb grazed in the spring sunshine. When I last visited Edward Brice he had a lot of pictures in his drawing-room, some framed, others still on easels. He told me, 'You know the auctioneer who sells in the cattle market?' I nodded, I knew him well. 'He has no idea of art.'

I was puzzled, not knowing what old Mr Brice, Tiddly Brice, was thinking. Then it came out. 'He sells pictures in heaps at furniture sales.'

'Oh!' I replied. 'You wouldn't like your pictures to be sold like that.'

I bought another picture from him but in the 1950s money was short and £10 was quite a speculation. Mr Brice died soon after and what he had dreaded happened. Apparently the remaining pictures in the house were sold by the cattle auctioneer who sold the furniture in lots.

Thinking back, Tiddly Brice knew full well that he was not popular with the villagers I know. But he enjoyed being just that. He talked to me as if he felt sorry for the non-artistic folk. They may have felt sorry for him in a funny way, and he certainly added to the variety of life in the village.

CHAPTER FIVE

CRICKETERS' FORUM

Some things run in families, so they say, but it's not often that we get four generations of wicket-keeper in one family. It happened at the village of Dumbleton on the edge of the Cotswolds.

The Hopkins family have lived in Dumbleton for many years. Back in the 1880s Edward Hopkins was a Dumbleton builder. In those days there was a very busy brickyard in the village, with bricks made from the blue clay of the vale. Edward Hopkins, known as Teddy Hopkins, built houses for the workers on the Dumbleton Estate. He also built the Baptist chapel at Ashton under Hill. I remember him as a little man who drove a governess cart around the villages, supervising his little team of workers. He kept wicket for Dumbleton on that hallowed turf near the church. I do know that Teddy Hopkins was a contemporary of my father.

Teddy had three sons, Eric, Leslie and Victor, all good cricketers. Victor was wicket-keeper in the Gloucestershire County side for a few years, when Walter Hammond was captain. Eric, the eldest son, kept wicket for Dumbleton. He was a big strapping chap with a very pleasing personality. He and his two brothers all played football for Ashton under Hill on a field called the Broadenham alongside Carrants Brook. Eric was centre-half and it took a good centre-forward to get past him. Eric farmed a small farm called Saberton for some years and then moved to Didcot Farm. In those days he farmed with horses and he did break in some useful animals.

In the next generation of the Hopkins family we come to Alec, who is an electrical contractor. He keeps wicket for Dumbleton too. In fact, he loves cricket and no doubt dreams of cricket. Alec is a 'cricketaholic', if there is such a word. He and his wife, Libby, have a farmhouse bed and breakfast establishment at Bengrove near Tewkesbury.

At Bengrove one is conscious that the simple life still exists. Bengrove Farm has hardly altered since I first knew it in the 1920s. To wake up on a June morning at Bengrove and hear the cuckoo in the wood, the mallard and moorhens on the pond and see the broad-breasted Aylesbury ducks strutting in the paddock is idyllic.

Alec's hobby, if it can be called a hobby, is rearing pheasants and partridges. It's a big part of life at Bengrove Farm, rather like a farm park in miniature. When the young pheasants are big enough they go into nearby woods and some are sent away to shoots in the country. Some of the young partridges go into a field of asparagus bower in the late summer. Alec's incubators, when I saw them, were a revelation to me because I'd only seen the young birds hatched under broody hens. Alec hatches both English and French partridges in the incubators. He says the English ones are better breeders and he may not hatch the Red Legged or French ones next year. Those chicks he does hatch he counts not in hundreds but in thousands.

Alec also keeps black retriever gun dogs, and shooting is another of his activities. Jane, Alec and Libby's daughter, has a Border collie bitch which has produced some super puppies, but the comedian of the household is a Jack Russell bitch called Pickle. Libby and Jane run a small flock of ewes on the field adjoining the farmhouse and Libby has been churchwarden at Teddington church and shows a great interest in village affairs.

Paul, the fourth generation of the Hopkins clan, now keeps wicket for Dumbleton and is a useful bowler when his dad is behind the stumps. Recently Dumbleton played a Cotswold team away from home. Alec was pleased that he had two stumpings and Paul took two wickets. They lost but as Alec said to me, it doesn't really matter losing the game, which was a good game. Coming back in the evening down Stanwey Hill was worth it all.

Bengrove Farm to me is one of the last survivors of village life and farming as I knew it some sixty-five years ago. There is no fancy talk of conservation, using chemical or artificial means. That has never been popular with this family. Everything is as nature intended.

What a family and what an oasis of peace.

CHAPTER SIX

GRAFTON AND JOHN DRINKWATER

The hamlet of Grafton, under Bredon Hill, has altered very little over the years. The lane up there is known as Lenchwick and as it curves round, hugging the hill, Churchway joins the Beckford Road. Villagers from the other parishes under the hill may smile at Grafton's little nest of houses where there is no pub, no school, no council estate, no shop and no church. There was a chapel of ease there, with a Norman archway, but this is now converted and the home of Mr Fred Mantle, son-in-law of William Coates, who was surely Grafton's guru and certainly a man of many talents.

William ran a little estate for the Ostler family. He prized himself on his goats. As almost everything he spoke of was to do with pedigree, he became known as Peddy Coates. Shoots on the estate were special in the winter months, when Peddy took on the role of a gamekeeper.

Peddy was shepherd for John Crump before he worked for the Ostlers. He must have known or at least seen most of the distinguished folk who lived in Grafton as well as those who were visiting, such as poets and musicians from the Midlands and further afield.

John Drinkwater, after a very unrewarding time in his life as an insurance clerk, became general manager of the theatre in Station Road, Birmingham, under Barry Jackson. He had already written some verse and paid a small bookseller to bring out a modest

35

volume of his poems. Some of his plays were performed at the Birmingham Repertory Theatre by The Pilgrim Players.

At weekends John travelled the country lanes on a second-hand bike, through the orchards of Worcestershire, the Malverns and the Cotswolds. He used to visit Grafton where he stayed at Upper Farm with the Ostler family, who were friends of mine. In 1913 he went with Rupert Brooke to stay at Dymock in Gloucestershire in a cottage owned by Lascelles Abercrombie. Here, joined by Wilfred Owen and Edward Thomas, they formed a group of poets.

I knew some of the Grafton Drinkwaters but not John. William Jubilee Drinkwater and his wife lived in a cottage near Crumps Farm. He was a coalman with a horse and dray. He had a mini wharf at Ashton under Hill station from where he delivered coal to the villages. The name Jubilee, of course, indicated that he was born in 1887, Queen Victoria's Golden Jubilee year.

John Drinkwater took a great interest in the rustic tunes of the local folk while he stayed at Grafton. In those far-off days before

The coalman making his deliveries

tape-recorders were even dreamed of, John sat in the bar of the Beckford Inn listening to the quaint songs of the pea-pickers and the gypsies. He jotted the words and tunes down in shorthand.

I wonder sometimes why John Drinkwater bothered to collect folk songs at the inn when he had such a gift for poetry himself. But like Cecil Sharp, John was deeply moved by the rural scene early in the century. His poem 'The Cotswold Farmers', a collection of half-truths, is most stimulating to read:

> Sometimes the ghosts forgotten go
> Along the hilltop way,
> And with long scythes of silver mow
> Meadows of moonlit hay.
> Until the cocks of Cotswold crow
> The coming of the day.
>
> There's Tommy Turtletob who died
> When he could drink no more;
> And Uncle Heretage, the pride
> Of eighteen twenty four,
> And Ebenezer Barleytide,
> And half a dozen more . . .
>
> They fold in phantom pens and plough
> Furrows without a share;
> And one will milk a fairy cow
> And one will stand and stare
> And whistle ghostly tunes that now
> Are not sung anywhere.
>
> The moon goes down on Oakridge lea,
> The other world's astir.
> The Cotswold farmers silently
> Go back to sepulchre.

The sleeping watchdogs wake and see
No ghostly harvester.

John Drinkwater described Grafton as no one else could have done in his poem 'At Grafton'. It's one of his more serious, contemplative writings, as he talks of the working hamlet with its golden thatch and crumbling stone:

God laughed when he made Grafton
That's under Bredon Hill.
A jewel in a jewelled plain.
The seasons work their will
On golden thatch and crumbling stone,
And every soft lipped breeze
Makes music for the Grafton men
In comfortable trees.

God's beauty over Grafton
Stole into roof and wall,
And hallowed every paved path
And every lowly stall.
And to a woven wonder
Conspired with one accord
The labour of the servant,
The labour of the Lord.

And momently to Grafton
Comes in from Vale and Wold
The sound of sheep unshepherded,
The sound of sheep in fold.
And, blown along the bases
Of lands that set their wide
Frank brows to God, comes chanting
The breath of Bristol Tide.

GRAFTON AND JOHN DRINKWATER

The days are good at Grafton,
The golden days and grey,
The busy clouds, the mellow barns,
And every winding way.
And oh, the peace of Grafton
Beneath the starlit skies,
God dreamt of when he fashioned
A woman's lovelit eyes.

CHAPTER SEVEN

GRAFTON AND DR L.P. JACKS

Harold Begbie was a typical Victorian evangelist. He wrote a book called *Broken Earthenware* and another called *Painted Windows*. He once had an interview with Dr Jacks, a Unitarian, but it proved to be a waste of time. Their religious views were too different. Dr Jacks said that he got rather bored with Begbie and suggested that they went and looked at a pen of pigs he was fattening. Begbie described Dr Jacks as an outdoor, thickset man with broad shoulders and an ivory face, all ploughed up and furrowed with mental strife.

As a philosopher, essayist and editor Dr Jacks was world famous. He was minister of the Church of the Messiah in Birmingham, which had among its congregation Joe Chamberlain, and Principal of Manchester College in Oxford, a centre of Unitarianism.

It was in 1897 that Dr Jacks came to Grafton and rented a farmhouse in the village. He was cycling around the Vale of Evesham and the Cotswolds when he saw the farmhouse, which the owner was willing to let at £20 per year. The house was on the south side of Bredon Hill, which slopes upwards from Grafton to a height of nearly 1,000 feet, with the Avon twisting snake-like through the valley below. He describes the orchards as a sea of blossom in springtime, in land where no bungalow or factory chimney can be seen.

This quote, from *Confessions of an Octogenarian* (George Allen and Unwin, 1942) by Dr Jacks, describes his views of his landlord, Fred Cormell, and of his time spent in the village.

My landlord, who lived in a neighbouring house, was a prosperous farmer. His name was Cormell, which sounded in local pronunciation rather like Cromwell and may have been a corruption of it. There was no reason to suppose him descended from my hero and fellow peasant, the Great Protector, though from the cut of him he might have been. My conversations with this man, as I sat with him in his kitchen with hams and flitches dangling above, and mugs of cider before us, were among the most illuminating I have had with any human being. Of intellect as we reckon it in Universities, he had not much; of education, reckoned likewise, nothing; but his stock of intuitions was amazing. From intercourse with this man I came to the conclusion that unless the soil and its cultivators are one soul and substance, so that each understands and loves the other, ill fares the land they cultivate, and ill fare the men who cultivate it – a point to be borne in mind by those who would accomplish the revival of British Agriculture. Being a peasant at heart it was not difficult for me to understand the elemental truths which emerged from the farmer's Cromwellian conversation.

Another friend of mine was a highly skilful shepherd employed by my landlord. As his master was a farmer in the sense that he was a living farm, so this man was a shepherd in the sense that he was a human sheep, or shall we say half sheep half man – a fertile combination. His voice distinctly reproduced a sheep's baa, and when he spoke to me I felt that a sheep was taking part in the conversation. But let no one suppose that this made it uninteresting. On the contrary I found it almost illuminating as that of his master, whose voice, as I have said, was as much the voice of a farm as of a farmer. There was unquestionably a sheep-element in that shepherd's mentality. How much wiser we should all be, our philosophers especially, for an occasional conversation with a sheep and how lucky was I to meet a man, like this shepherd, who could translate the sheep's language into Gloucestershire dialect. When I began to write books, which I did largely under the influence of these surroundings, I combined him into a composite image with another shepherd of my acquaintance, and put it into a book called *Mad Shepherds* under the name Snarley Bob.

These and such like were my companions during the twenty years when this place was my holiday home. They served to enrich my conception of the Common Man and to strengthen my belief in him as the Messiah, the appointed saviour of society and the completer of the Reformation. One effect of this, I believe, was to improve the quality of my Birmingham Preaching, which needed improving. The improvement consisted in a nearer approach to reality and less concern with distant views of it, my own or other men's.

It was good also for my six children, who ran wild over the country, with the police occasionally after them for minor offences against the law, learnt to fend for themselves, as their elders did; learnt also that the food they ate and the milk they drank were not mere shop articles whose history began when they were bought over the counter or deposited at the kitchen door. They caught fish in the stream and cooked them; they rode horses and broke their bones; they watched the pressing of cider and the brewing of mead, both domestic products, and found by experiment that if they sampled either of these beverages too freely it would make them drunk. Their subsequent walk and conversation gives me no reason to believe that these lessons were thrown away.

Meanwhile I digged, planted, kept bees, bred livestock and spread their dung over the grateful earth, the vegetable congregations responding to my ministries as no human congregation had ever done, perhaps recognising that a peasant was the minister. The crops flourished, the animals brought forth, the flowers laughed in their beds, and all night long in her season the nightingale sang her amorous descant round my dwelling place. I now perceived more clearly than ever that the Power-not-

Middle Farm, Grafton, the country home of Dr Jacks

ourselves makes for other things besides righteousness, though perhaps included within it on a right definition of that term. It makes, I thought, for courage, often challenging to combat those to whom it loves, adopting them as sons if they fight well, but pursuing them with hailstones and coals of fire if they run away, its love all turned to hate. All which may be found written in The Book of the Word of the Lord.

43

And so it went on till the time came for Harold Begbie to interview me on my 'religious views', and for me to break off the conversation by inviting him to take a look at my fat pigs, and to find myself consequentially placed in a stained glass window, with a good guess at my character written below.

As I read and read again Dr Jacks' assessment of Fred Cormell I'm amazed at the philosophy of a man who calls himself a peasant. I knew Fred Cormell but Dr Jacks has opened my eyes to qualities of this Cromwellian farmer that I didn't realize he had. Cormell came to a farm known as News Farm at Ashton under Hill late in the last century. Before then he had been a farm bailiff at or near Cropthorne. The old saying about bailiffs is that they mix the sugar with the sand. When stock goes to market some is booked in the owner's name, some in the bailiff's. Whether that happened in Fred's case I don't know. What I do know is that he came to News Farm, bought it, and was a good farmer. He soon changed the name of the farm to The Manor to enhance its value.

Fred Cormell's carter told me innumerable stories about him. He fancied himself as district councillor, but would have to stand against Doctor Roberson. Doctor Roberson was well thought of by rich and poor alike. He was a man of the people, and had represented the village unopposed for years. Fred Cormell researched his chances of beating the doctor in the election. 'Right,' he thought, 'I'll talk to the young men in the Star Inn.'

'Do you want land for allotments?' he questioned.

'Oh yes Sir, we do, badly,' one man replied and seven of them agreed.

Fred Cormell offered to let them have a field up on Bredon Hill for allotments if they would vote for him in the district council election. So the men cleared the gorse off the hill. They borrowed Fred Cormell's horses to plough the land on Saturday afternoons and planted their crops. But Doctor Roberson beat Fred at the election, and he took back the land from the young allotment holders. What is the field known as today? It is called The Promised Land.

Fred was a very tight customer with his money. In those days Dad was a member of the Salvation Army. He went to News Farm once, collecting for the Army. First of all he saw Fred's housekeeper, explaining to her what good work the Army did among the poor. She gave my father a shilling, a very generous contribution at the turn of the century. Then Fred invited Dad into the small sitting-room where he spent his winter evenings.

'Oh, Tom. You're collecting for a good cause I see. I'll subscribe to that.' He rattled his money in his trouser pocket while Dad explained the good work the Army did in the slums of London. 'I'm sure they do, Tom, it's a good cause.'

Dad took his book from his pocket saying, 'How much, Mr Cormell?'

'Put me down for tuppence,' came the reply.

Fred Cormell, however, was generous to Dad and rented 15 acres of farm land to him to grow peas. His prowess as a farmer and stock-breeder was known in the Evesham vale. He had a fine stable of horses under his carter, Tom Whittle. Fat cattle were taken regularly to the local market. He said that one summer, out of just one field, he sold £1,000 worth of fat bullocks, which was a lot of money at that time.

At one stage in his farming career Fred Cormell advertised in the local paper for a workman. A fellow came from a nearby village and applied for the position. After some conversation between the potential master and man, Fred Cormell said, 'I want you to bring me references of your character.'

At his dinner in the village pub the man told the customers that he had applied to work for Mr Cormell. All sorts of stories were told about Fred, some true, others far-fetched. The man decided that News Farm cottage was not for him. Going back to see Mr Cormell, he was asked 'Have you got your references?'

'No,' the man replied, 'but I have got thine, and I'm not coming.'

Fred's cows came every morning and night along the grass verge beside Mrs Ford's house. They made rather a mess of the grass in winter and Mrs Ford tackled him about it.

'People who live in glasshouses shouldn't throw stones,' Fred replied. 'Just keep your hens out of my rick-yard, scratching my chaff and mangolds in the cows' mangers.' Some said that Mrs Ford wished she had not complained.

One of the other characters in Dr Jacks' book *Mad Shepherds* was Snarley Bob, a man we all knew of course. Snarley Bob, as described

Snarley Bob the shepherd lived in Norman Cottage, Grafton

by Jacks, was an old man when I first met him. He wore his hair long, had long bushy eyebrows and whiskers. I wouldn't say he had a beard, just whiskers. He was a woolley man, like the sheep he had once shepherded. I knew him as a goatherd, though, with a number of milking goats. I remember Snarley milking the goats as they stood on wooden platforms with the cards of the prizes they had won nailed on the goatshed wall. It's true, Snarley Bob was the spirit of Grafton.

Our land adjoined Mr Ostler's, half-way up Bredon Hill. In the summer it was the job of Frank and me to count our cattle on a field known as The Leasowe. Snarley made a complaint that one of our heifers had been in Ostler's field for more than a week. We met him on the hill and Frank called him a liar, and we had to go to Grafton to apologize.

As well as being a philosophizer, writer and great observer of people, Doctor Jacks was a keen gardener and had a passion for the soil. As he said, 'I want to do something with it for, after all, I am going back to the soil in the end.'

When Dr Jacks made his first beehive and procured a swarm of bees from Mr Jonathan Bayliss, who lived at Paris on Bredon slopes, he knew nothing of bees. That was typical of the man. By 1916 Dr Jacks had thirty-six hives which he kept in a small walled garden close to his house at Middle Farm. At one time the bees took over the garden and the whole family were stung, but Dr Jacks became immune to the sting of his bees. The bees were an Italian variety and very busy. In thundery weather they would become angry, like all bees do.

Adjoining Dr Jacks' garden was a meadow belonging to Fred Cormell. In late June at the time of the Pershore Fair, the 26th of the month, Fred had the meadow mown for hay. Tom Whittle, the young carter, sized the job up on the Sunday evening as he walked from Ashton. The bees were everywhere on the meadow, taking pollen from the wild white clover. Tom thought and concluded that if he took his two horses and the mowing machine into the meadow, both he and his horses would be stung.

At just after three o'clock on the Monday morning, as it was just getting light in those days before British Summer Time was introduced, Tom's two-horse team circled the meadow with the mower. The heavy dew drenched their hooves as the grass fell before the mower's blades. As the sun peeped over the Cotswold edge, Tom's horses had already mown a wide headland. By breakfast time the field had been mown and Tom and his horses were resting under the hedge far away from Dr Jacks' garden, his apple trees, and his bees. Fred Cormell walked across the meadow kicking the swathes of new-mown hay with his feet, pleased no doubt that Tom had mown the field and I think appreciating full well why it had been done so early in the morning.

The two men started to chat. 'Morning Tom.'

'Morning Gaffer.'

Fred said, with a snigger, 'Couldn't you sleep last night then Tom? What was up of you this morning?'

Tom replied, 'I knew what I was about and wanted this job done before them warm-arsed 'uns, Master Jacks' bees, got up. Neither I nor your 'osses were stung.'

'Good lad Tom,' replied Fred. 'I never thought you had it in you.'

Two men who lived at Ashton did not escape Dr Jacks' bees. They could be described as sleeping rough in one of Fred Cormell's barns, and their initial problem was cider, not bees. They were always what the locals termed as about three parts, well over the present-day breathalyser limit. Their names were Nailus Allen and Spider Winnet. Working for Dr Jacks one day, and a little more than three parts drunk on cider, they were asked to move some empty beehives from the garden and put them under the hedge. By mistake they caught hold of a hive full of bees, fell over with it and pulled it on top of them. They both got badly stung but it did sober them up.

One thing that strikes me quite forcibly is how Dr Jacks, a product of city life when he came to Gloucestershire under Bredon

Hill, was more of a countryman than many of the natives who had lived their for centuries. He had an open mind, and made his assessments of the natural world in an uninhibited manner.

Dr Jacks did nothing by halves. He planted 100 fruit trees on land across the road from the house and in 1900, a good year for fruit, he sold six 72 pound pots of Victoria plums, six pots of Cox's Emperor plums. I remember those fruit trees and I must say I have never since seen Victoria plums of the superb quality grown at Grafton.

In 1889 Dr Jacks married Olive Cecelia, the daughter of Revd Stopford Brooks. She was a beautiful woman and was the model for the famous painting 'The Gardener's Daughter', although in reality she became 'the gardener's wife'.

Dr Jacks and his family led a kind of gypsy life, trekking backwards and forwards from Birmingham to their country paradise at Grafton. They stayed at Middle Farm for ten days at New Year, three weeks at Easter, and six weeks in the summer, while the doctor and his wife made weekly visits, sometimes just for a day starting early and getting back to Birmingham late, sometimes for one or two nights. They often walked the 5 miles from Evesham late at night and then back to Evesham the following night to catch the Birmingham train, and sometimes Dr Jacks cycled the 36 miles from the city.

At weekends and during long holidays Grafton proved to be an idyllic spot. For a large family with six children like the Jacks, the holiday home was ideal. The children could wander where they liked on Bredon Hill, away from the city streets of Birmingham. There were some drawbacks in these days before the telephone kiosk stood opposite the front gate of Middle Farm. When a doctor was needed someone bicycled the 1½ miles to Ashton station and sent a telegram message for the doctor who lived 6 miles away. But that was a rare event.

Sometimes the family set up night lines to catch eels at Carrant Brook and they would be away before breakfast to check the lines, the young Jacks skinning the catch for the cook. There was so much to interest the family, including cricket in the farmyard and bird-watching. Dr Jacks had an old flintlock gun he bought at a sale. He made lead bullets for it, primed it, loaded it and fired it across the farmyard.

When the family made its thrice-yearly trip to Grafton it meant not only transporting six children and two or three enormous travelling trunks stuffed with the family bedding and clothes, but also a nanny, a cook and a maid. There were chickens to move in hampers, a rabbit, and a bullfinch. At Ashton railway station 1½ miles from Middle Farm little Martin Hawker would meet the train with a handcart. Martin, a man described as 'five foot and a tater', was a loyal servant in the Jacks' household. I knew him well, a skilled farm worker. I recall how his nose twitched as he spoke and his voice was rather high pitched. A picture of him comes to mind dressed in cords, wearing a billy cock hat in winter and a battered straw hat at harvest. I've seen him build corn ricks which looked as permanent as the thatched cottage he lived in. When the machine came in winter to thresh the corn it seemed a pity to pull the structure apart.

On Sunday nights in summer Martin swapped his cords for a grey suit and worshipped at St Barbara's church along with Bill Spires. Together they made a picture of rural simplicity.

When the Jacks family moved to Oxford Dr Jacks had two riding horses and at the end of the summer he rode one back to the city. The boys followed on bikes, the full 50 miles. The little caravan of travellers stopped for the night at the Merrymouth Inn near Burford.

In 1916 Dr Jacks moved from Grafton to his permanent home in Oxford. By then the trees which he had planted in the garden over the road were half-grown. He wanted them at his garden in Headington. Martin dug up the trees, wrapped their roots in sacking, and transported them to Beckford station in one of John Crump's wagons. They were then transferred to a railway truck, bound for Headington in Oxfordshire. I can well imagine that Martin had to make many journeys with the wagon to move 100 trees. He then travelled to Headington, unloaded the trees and planted them on Dr Jacks' land. Of course they grew, for Martin had been meticulous in their digging up and replanting. He was a pixie of a man, a true son of the soil like his master, Dr Jacks.

CHAPTER EIGHT

ANNIE SPIRES, PROFESSOR ALFRED HAYES AND SIR GRANVILLE BANTOCK

Annie Spires, like most girls at the end of the last century went out to service. She was thirteen years of age when she was sent to work in the Birmingham house of Professor Alfred Hayes, scholar, writer and dramatist. His country house in Grafton was opposite the thatched cottage which was once a small church. The Norman arch of its former chancel can still be seen. It was built apparently by the monks of Beckford Priory.

During the Boer War John Crump, who farmed Manor Farm, Grafton, had several harvest homes in Dr Jacks' big barn. These were memorable occasions to Annie. Her grandfather, Charles Spires, born in 1812, used to recite the following at these suppers:

> All ye rakish farmers that stay up late at night,
> Mind when you go to bed choose some candle light.
> Now Betty, you go up to bed
> And I'll stay up tonight instead.

He then gave the toast:

Charles Spires, Crump's shepherd, was born in 1812

The plough and the flail,
The fleece and the frail,
Not forgetting the milking pail.

Charles' son William played tunes on a melodeon while the songs sung included 'The Spotted Cow' and 'The Sweet Nightingale'. Shepherds, carters and cowmen all joined in, helped by plenty of good cider from John Crump's Black Taunton trees.

Annie always struck me as someone with quality and a special grace. This she obtained not from some classy school or college but from working in the houses of folk of quality. When I visited her, the grace and charm amazed me. Every little move in her cottage living-room was that of a lady.

'I want to show you something,' she whispered to me once, as if she were about to share some secret with me. From a blanket box she produced linen sheets, woollen blankets and yards of red flannel. 'These are what Mother and I bought with our Mumping Money.'

Then Annie told me of the hard times at the beginning of the century when she went mumping with her widowed mother. Mumping Day was St Thomas's Day, 21 December, the shortest day of the year. Poor people went around the big houses in the village of Grafton and Beckford, reciting 'Bud well, bear well, God send fare well. A bushel of apples to give on St Thomas's morning.' The mumpers and their children were given mince pies, home-made wine, and apples besides money to buy clothes. In the village school Smith Bros, who kept the shop, had warm winter blankets and clothes laid out on trestle-tables to sell to the mumpers. Annie looked after these items and showed them to me proudly.

Professor Hayes often went for a day's trout fishing in the Elan Valley accompanied by his good friend Sir Granville Bantock. Annie smiled when she told me how they brought their day's catch back to the house in Birmingham for her to cook for their supper.

Alfred Hayes loved his country house at Grafton under Bredon Hill where Sir Granville was a frequent visitor. Professor Hayes translated drama in verse from Pushkin. His other works include *A Fellowship of Song*, an historical drama about Simon de Montford who was killed in the Battle of Evesham in 1265. I imagine that Alfred Hayes was able to put extra atmosphere into this drama as he only lived 6½ miles from the Evesham battlefield.

Alfred Hayes, however, was much more than just a dramatist and writer. The great man loved his garden and tutored his students in Russian on the lawn. If the weather was chilly he would wrap a plaid blanket around his shoulders. His costume dramas were often rehearsed in his garden to the delight of the people of the hamlet. Men like Martin Hawker, Bill Spires and William Coates were taken aback by what they saw. These folk had never been further afield than the market towns of Evesham and Tewkesbury.

The hill above Grafton was a classroom where Alfred Hayes studied another interest – geology. The sea once covered the hill and star shell fossils could be found in the quarries. The life that Hayes enjoyed most was a simple life, mixing with the real people of the countryside, farmers and labourers alike, all of whom felt equally at home in his company.

Mrs Hayes had a lovely singing voice and would sing for hours to the accompaniment of Sir Granville Bantock on the grand piano. Sir Granville enjoyed particular distinction as a composer and conductor and was highly regarded for his skill in orchestration. He regarded himself as an individualist and didn't worry in the least about the popular music of the day. He wrote his 'Helena Variations for Orchestra' in honour of his wife and she had some of her verses set to music by him. Sibelius dedicated his Third Symphony to Sir Granville.

It was Sir Granville who amused young Annie Spires as he improvised on the piano. She was cooking in the kitchen and heard the pulse of the music softly whispered from the drawing-room as he played a new setting, one two three four, one two three four. His son practised on the bagpipes in the lane outside. Can you

Binding work in progress in the fields at Grafton

imagine the comments. Had ever such an instrument been heard in Grafton before?

What colourful personalities these two were. Alfred Hayes' house was a delightful spot under Bredon Hill where he grew rare plants and flowers and planted a walnut tree. And the tree still stands, a sentinel at the corner of the lane, a memory of life before the First World War.

CHAPTER NINE

MEN OF THE CLOTH

Parsons, Nonconformist ministers and local preachers have always intrigued me, having listened in fear and trepidation to some of these men as they preached on Hell Fire till one could almost smell the brimstone. But now things have changed. Preaching is a lost art. Some of the old style of exponents of the Gospel were real entertainers, although some were deadly dull.

In the last century, in Grandfather's day, the parson of Beckford and Ashton under Hill was none other than the Revd Dr John Timbrell. His ministry there lasted from 1797 until his death in 1865 at the age of ninety-seven, and his sixty-eight years as vicar were still remembered by a few parishioners when I was a boy.

Susan Vale of Grafton lived to be an old lady. She recalled that when Timbrell passed through the village with his coach and pair driven by his coachman, she and the other little girls were expected to curtsey to him. The men were expected to raise their hats or they were in trouble. The farm workers, hearing the wheels of Timbrell's coach as it came along Beckford's Way, would down their tools and hide under the hedge.

John Timbrell was Archdeacon of Gloucester Cathedral and, as Revd Witts in his *Diary of a Cotswold Parson* explains, he was a strong-headed, intelligent, active man and a leading magistrate in the county.

At one time John Timbrell held the living at Bretforton, a village at the foot of the Cotswolds and a portrait of him hangs in the vestry at Bretforton church. When the rule was made that a parson had to live in the parish Timbrell had two livings, and decided to move to Beckford Vicarage. At Beckford he added several wings to the house, which to my mind rather spoilt it. In Timbrell's day there was a court held at Beckford and he presided over the Petty Sessions there.

One of Timbrell's cases involved a Grafton boy (according to Sue Vale), who had been scrumping apples in an orchard. He was brought before Judge Timbrell and explained, 'I did it for a lark, Sir.'

Timbrell replied, 'We have a cage for larks at Gloucester.'

An Ashton man sentenced by him was sent to Northleach Jail and put on the treadmill. He returned to his village a physical wreck. Timbrell once even sentenced a Cheltenham man to transportation to Australia. There seems no doubt that this man of the cloth was a martinet.

Revd Witts attended the Archdeacon's visitation at Stow-on-the-Wold in May 1826 and wrote:

> Dr Timbrell preached a good, moderate sermon on the duties of the Christian Ministry, which would have been more useful had it been less general. His vehement and authoritative manner on one or two occasions both to the Church Warden and the clergy, to the latter on the subject of apologies for not attending being omitted by some absent encumbents and curates, excited a little prejudice against him. His principle was right, his manner of explaining wrong.

In August 1825 Timbrell preached a long sermon before the Judges of Gloucester Assizes. His text was 'Be quiet and study to do your own business'. He exhorted men to personal reformation, loyalty, obedience and submission to the laws.

Half-way through John Timbrell's ministry at Beckford he was asked to conduct a wedding early in the morning. A couple were to be married in a hurry by licence. They needed a witness for the ceremony. John Timbrell told his son that he would be needed at the church at an early hour to act as witness. The bride and groom arrived at the church, and Revd Timbrell went to his son's bedroom to waken him in time for the wedding. The son had been out drinking heavily the night before. Timbrell tried to waken him, but to no avail. He was dead, having choked on his vomit. The Revd Timbrell looked at his son saying, 'Can't help you but I must attend to the wedding.' He scoured Beckford village for a replacement, finding a tramp in his stable to witness the wedding.

When Timbrell died in 1865 he was followed by the Revd Joseph Harrison. Harrison was a different kettle of fish. He mixed with the common people and was good to the poor. There was nothing autocratic about Joseph. His only failing was that he was a heavy drinker.

During his ministry Harrison presided over a school in the church vestry. The school was later housed at Stanley Farm, where

The parson and clerk

I was born and farmed for thirty years. My uncle Jim attended Sunday school in the church. He said that when the Reverend Gentleman had had too much to drink, Sunday school didn't last long.

Harrison's theme, Uncle said, was 'Don't do as I do, do as I tell you'. Grandfather rented 4 acres of Glebe land at Carrants Field and Revd Harrison used to collect the rent, the field being the property of the church. Sometimes owing to his excessive drinking and his benevolence to the poor he got short of money. He would go and see Grandfather on his holding, where he had what is known as a hovel to keep his tools and an adjoining stable for his donkey. Revd Harrison would come to see him there on occasions to sample Grandfather's home-made wine.

'I've come for the rent, William, if you can let me have it,' he said. 'I know it's not due yet but pay me now and I'll make an allowance for that.'

'It's due on Lady Day and it's only just turned Christmas,' Grandfather replied.

And Revd Harrison knocked £1 off the rent.

At a wedding at St Barbara's church at Ashton Revd Harrison was conducting the ceremony. Unfortunately he was well over the limit and got mixed up. To everyone's horror he began conducting the funeral service. He apologized afterwards and explained that his trouble was that he was so moved by the Spirit – the wrong 'spirit' I guess. But despite his weakness Revd Joseph Harrison was a good man, a friend of the poor and a man of the people.

He was followed in 1895 by Revd John Gough, a High Church man and a scholar. He came at a time when tolerance between the Church of England and Nonconformity was almost non-existent. Revd Gough suited the few upper-class folk in the village but he treated the farm labourers like peasants.

My cousin Percy died as a new-born baby. He died without being baptized and Gough refused to bury him in St Barbara's churchyard. This did create a problem for my uncle and aunt. Dad

The Revd Margetts and the church choir

at that time had a Bradbury motor bike and sidecar and he fetched the Baptist minister from Evesham to bury Percy.

What a contrast when Revd William John Margetts arrived in 1912. Here was a wonderful pastor and friend to one and all, loved by the villagers, a true and compassionate Christian. He stayed until his death in 1924.

Revd W.W. Baker, who came from Birmingham to be vicar, I would describe as a man and a half, a sort of Baring-Gould of Worcestershire. There were so many facets to Baker. He had a good voice and would sing at concerts, songs such as 'Tomorrow will be Friday and we must eat Fish Today.' He worked well with the chapel folk, and what an appetite this man had. At village teas, known as bun fights, the ladies saw to it that a plate of doughnuts was put on the table in front of Revd Baker.

At a bell ringers supper he said, 'I'd like to see the ringers at the church service sometimes.'

The captain of the tower replied, 'Oh, I'd like to see the vicar with us in the belfry.'

But it was all good humoured. When the supper was put before the men Revd Baker, at the head of the table, got started on the meal straightaway. One of the churchwardens said, 'Mr Baker, we have not said Grace yet.'

'Oh, I'm awfully sorry,' he replied. 'The sight of this lovely food made me forget that item.'

Revd Baker lived to be over a hundred. When a newspaper reporter interviewed him and asked to what he attributed his longevity, he replied, 'Fish and chips with plenty of salt and vinegar.'

This jovial man excelled at funerals. He always had something good to say about the deceased, however they had lived their lives.

Revd Baker had a special sense of humour. He told me once how he had drunk wine from a teapot when visiting one lady. She said it looked better. When he visited folk who were ill he took them a tin of cocoa but always asked them to open it while he was there because he collected the coupons.

On a visit to Shepherd Tidmarsh he reminded the shepherd that he had a flock much the same as his. 'How many sheep have you, Shepherd?' he inquired.

The old man thought a minute and replied, 'Over two hundred ewes and their lambs. How about you then, Vicar, your flock?'

Revd Baker said that there were about nine hundred altogether. Four hundred at Ashton and five hundred at Beckford. Tidmarsh too had a sense of humour and was not going to be outdone by the vicar's larger flock. He had been ill for some time, and this was the vicar's first visit.

'I'll tell you what, Vicar,' he began, 'if I didn't go round my flock of sheep any more often than you do, shouldn't I get some maggots!'

The two shepherds laughed over this as they drank some of Mrs Tidmarsh's beetroot wine until their faces shone like beetroots too. Revd W.W. Baker was an ideal village parson. I doubt we will see his like again.

CHAPTER TEN

WALTER GREEN AND BREDON HILL

Anyone who knew Walter Green would agree that he was one of the most colourful characters around Bredon Hill. First of all he knew the hill like the back of his hand. All the old tracks were as familiar to him as the motorways are to a long distance lorry driver of today. He once told me how a farmer from Elmley Castle drove his horse and cart every month over the hill to Beckford Market. I never knew quite why, for the road around the hill through Ashton was quite direct.

Walter was a naturalist in a way. He was fond of the wild birds and beasts, but he was a trapper as well. A line, a fine line, had been drawn by this remarkable man in his youth, a demarcation between the birds and beasts which were to be preserved and those he thought harmful. In the outhouse at the back of his cottage, hung on pegs and nails, were various traps to catch vermin or 'varmints', as he called them. There were traps to set on gateposts for hawks, snares for badgers, gin traps for rabbits, all commonplace sixty years ago, as well as bullet moulds and powder flasks for his muzzle loader guns.

For much of his life Walter was a pig farmer, keeping his sows and weaners in a paddock at the back of his cottage. He had strong views about how pigs should be fed and like his contemporaries he was a great believer in fat bacon.

'Now the bacon you get today,' he would say, ''tis never cured, just soaked in brine. If you need to fry an egg the only way is to use lard. No, there's not enough fat in it to fry an egg.'

'Now when I kept Gloucester Old Spots out yer,' he continued, pointing his finger at the old paddock, 'we allus had one in the house for Christmas. A big 'un mind, there was something to cut at then a day.'

'You used to play cricket didn't you, Walter?' I questioned.

He straightened his cap, then held an imaginary ball in his left hand and swung his arm round in the kitchen, saying, 'They used to call me Bumper at cricket.'

'Why was that?' I asked, having a good idea. The reason for his name was a legend around the vale.

'It all started one Saturday at Overbury,' he said. 'We were playing the Cheltenham Police. 'Twas the hot summer of 1921, the ground was as hard as the Devil's back teeth. Percy Attwood, our Captain, asked me to open the bowling. The first ball I bowled dropped short on a plantain and it hit the Police Sergeant in the jowls.'

I looked puzzled. 'But surely jowls are connected with pigs,' I said.

'Ah,' he replied, ''tis under the jaw bone. He went down like a stone and lay there and showed the whites of his eyes as they carried him off.'

'A young bobby came in next and my ball just skimmed his temples as he ducked. "Walter," Percy Attwood called from behind the sticks, "send the next few balls in this over down steady and that will do for today. A fellow was killed at Ashton the other Saturday." Percy put the slow bowlers on then for I was too dangerous.'

I visited Walter one winter afternoon a few years ago. He had just come out of the garden.

'Sit yourself down, I be just going to have a swill,' he announced.

I sat down by a roaring fire and listened to the noise of buckets and bowls as he lathered himself, stripped to the waist. He came from the wash-house to the kitchen towelling himself, as clean as a new pin.

Out in the garden I remarked on the cold wind. Walter explained, "Tis the skinny wind from Russia; nothing to stop it between here and the Ural Mountains.'

'How's your arthritis, Walter?'

'Oh, it's no better. It's the oil that dries up in the joints and the bones graunches together.'

What a good description I thought.

'I suppose you must expect something when you are over eighty,' I said.

In a crack came the reply: 'You get it whether you expect it or not.'

Walter had been a strong, rugged man but he once had a spell in hospital. I visited him there and when he returned to his cottage he told me, 'I said to the doctor, "The longer you keep me here the harder it will be for me to cope at home."'

Walter died the following year and he left word with the vicar that he would like me to read the lesson at his funeral. It included the words, 'And he saw a new heaven and a new earth, for the first heaven and the first earth were passed away.' They seemed fitting for Walter, a true son of the soil. For me it seemed that a link with the Victorians had gone with him.

Thinking back, I remember Walter Green as the Uncle Silas of Bredon Hill. That 'skinny wind' from Russia still blows across the vale to chill Pigeon Lane where Walter lived.

On the north-west side of Bredon Hill the ground is different from the cold clay on the north-east. The land is earlier, easier to work, but the slope of the hill has only 5 inches of soil over limestone. Although the land could be described as poor agricultural land, men with brains, capital and energy had turned 130 acres of this hill-side into a fruit farm.

In the 1920s, if used for agricultural purposes, it would be difficult to find employment for three men on this land. Under fruit, however, the Overbury Estate, who owned the land, employed forty men, women and boys permanently, together with the population of two villages at picking time. Research by experts from Long Ashton near Bristol was valuable and the work done by Mr Raymond Bush, who achieved so much in his study of spring frosts, guided the land owners in their planting of the hill. Frosts in the spring when the trees blossom are a problem for fruit growers. Raymond Bush was one of the first to recognize the fact that spring frosts settle in valleys while the hills are often free. The hills do have the problem of cold east winds scorching the fruit blossom and he advised wind-breaks to solve this menace. Growing in only 5 inches of soil, the apple trees had no tap root but spread their roots laterally. Some of the finest Cox's Orange apples grew on Bredon Hill just before the 1939 war. They were sold in shops owned by the estate at Weston-super-Mare and other seaside resorts. Strawberries, gooseberries, plums, raspberries, black- and redcurrants were all a part of the Bredon Hill enterprise.

On the rabbit-infested summit of Bredon Hill other enterprises were afoot. Mr Hosier, the Wiltshire farmer, had introduced two new ventures for farmers. The Overbury Estate's progressive farmers invested in bail milking on Bredon Hill with a herd of Shorthorn cows and a Hereford bull, a profitable feature on the well-drained hill land. Hosier's milking bail was moved every day on to fresh land, its milking machine powered by a petrol engine becoming a feature on the hill. The cows seemed happy with the cake rations and grazing the land and there were no problems with muck carting!

Hosier's next idea was folding units for laying hens. These arks held twenty-four birds and were moved daily on to fresh pasture; the scratching of the hens and the manure improved the hill land immensely. Poor land became productive and men and women were given gainful employment.

To be on Bredon Hill on a winter's night and see the moon rise over the frosty landscape is a magical experience. Something inexplicable is conjured up in the mind by the expression 'the sound of silence', but it's real! I used to like to listen to the stillness

A summer picnic on Bredon

of winter, only interrupted by the call of the tawny owl, which forecast a fine day, and the distant muted clatter of a labouring goods train puffing its way from Avonmouth and Bristol to Birmingham with a load of bananas.

But Bredon in spring and summer is a place apart. Then the cry of the peewits, nesting behind the firs by the quarry, goes on and on. When the young birds hatch in the scooped-out nest on the arable land the parents do such a good job as decoys, crying some distance away from the nest to detract any humans from finding it. All day long the larks perform their vertical take-off and twitter high above the hill. On the banks of the quarry the wild thyme grows.

On the summit Parsons Folly, built by Squire Parsons in 1795, is 40 foot high. It turns the 960 foot hill into a 1,000 foot mountain. William Cobbett wrote of the hill in his *Rural Rides*. Although *Rural Rides* is full of rather extreme utterances, one quotation relating to Bredon Hill does please me:

> From Bredon Hill you can see into nine or ten counties and those curious bubblings up, the Malvern Hills, are right before you. You certainly see from this hill one of the richest spots in England and I am convinced there is no richer spot anywhere in the world, Scotland excepted.

Walter Green knew the custodian of the Folly very well, the hermit I met as a boy. Walter told me of a pig the hermit kept in a barn, which was his home too. It was a Gloucester Old Spot that he had bought off Walter. Stories are legion of the hermit living off the hill on rabbits, mushrooms, everything in season.

When Squire Parsons visited London in the late eighteenth century one of the cries he heard in the streets was 'Bredon Hill rabbits'. They were famous for their size and flavour, the heaviest and tastiest you could buy.

Housman's poem 'Summer Time on Bredon' sums up the picture of the hill. A hill where on Sunday mornings the sound of bells from the village churches was music to the ears of folk like Walter in Pigeon Lane with his pigs, Gamekeeper Joe at Cobblers Quar, and the Hermit.

> In Summer Time on Bredon
> The bells they ring so clear;
> Round both the Shires they ring them
> In steeples far and near,
> A happy noise to hear.
>
> Here of a Sunday morning
> My love and I would lie,
> And see the coloured counties,
> And hear the larks so high
> About us in the sky.

The bells would ring to call me
In valleys miles away;
'Come all to church, good people;
Good people, come and pray.'
But here my love would stay.

And I would turn and answer
Among the springing thyme,
'Oh, peal upon our wedding,
And we will hear the chime,
And come to church on time.'

But when the snows at Christmas
On Bredon top were strown,
My love rose up so early
And stole out unbeknown
And went to church alone.

They tolled the one bell only,
Groom there was none to see,
The mourners followed after,
And so to church went she,
And would not wait for me.

The bells they sound on Bredon,
And still the steeples hum,
'Come all to church, good people,'
Oh, noisy bells, be dumb;
I hear you, I will come.

CHAPTER ELEVEN

THE ROYAL DUKES AT EVESHAM

Mr B.G. Cox, Chairman of Evesham Historical Society, in which I served as a committee member, wrote a book entitled *Wood Norton*. It is a brief account of the estate and its occupiers and of the Bourbon-Orleans family of the Royal House of France who lived there. I'm deeply indebted to him for letting me dip into his research. Ben is a historian and now curator of Blandford Museum.

When the Duc d'Aumarle first arrived at Wood Norton in 1857 he expected that one day soon he would be called back to his rightful place in a restored French monarchy, for he was the son of the deposed King Louis Phillipe of France. Wood Norton in those days was a modest country house, more of a shooting lodge, but for the duke it was a place of refuge from all the turmoil in France.

The Duc d'Aumarle rented the estate from Edward Holland, Squire of Dumbleton, the last Liberal MP for Evesham. The duke soon had large estates in Worcestershire and in the Cotswolds. His land at Taddington, near Cutsdean, had as its tenant old Charles Cook who ran a pack of harriers there.

An exile from France, the duke had no option but to hunt the hare as the Cotswold acres had been divided up for fox hunting long ago. Various packs of hounds hunted the fox between age-old boundaries drawn by parishes, brooks and woods. Hare hunting was an older sport but the field, or followers, were looked upon as an inferior set. The huntsmen who wielded the whip were dressed in sober green jackets and white breeches. A farmer in his tweeds was more the type to be seen with the harriers. The hounds were often mismarked fox hounds, smaller and not so matching. Hares were plentiful in the late nineteenth century on those bleak windswept Cotswold hills. No doubt many Cotswold men followed on foot to see the duke's pack harry and catch the Cotswold hare.

Hares have a habit of keeping within their own territory. They run in circles around a few fields, so by standing on a knoll, or a knolp as a Cotswold man would say, the chase could be watched without a lot of walking. How different Sally the hare from Reynard the fox, who will run with the wind in his brush taking a straight line from covert to covert. When the motley crowd met in a farmyard the duke led his pack with H.H. Stephenson, who played cricket for Worcestershire, as huntsman. They found their first hare in Mr Cook's turnip field. Hares often made for a farm gate or perhaps a narrow bridle gate when chased from one field to another; they seldom made long runs on those hills. With ears laid low, using her hind legs like a miniature kangaroo, Sally gave the harriers such a good run that one must wonder how the Duc d'Aumarle became such a successful Master of Hare Hounds on those Cotswold hills.

Old Charles Cook of Taddington reconciled being a true yeoman of England and a tenant of the French duke very well. He was a man of many parts: a breeder of excellent horses and valiant sons; a hill farmer of repute; a rhyme writer; a dispenser of fine port wine; and he knew and enjoyed the best things a successful agriculturalist and good sportsman could have with the duke as his landlord.

A magazine of the day recalls how Charles entertained the foreign gentry, who were affectionately known as the Royal Carrant Jelly boys. The hunt breakfast over and the toasts drunk Charles Cook rose to his feet to make an address.

'My Noble Princes of France, Earls, Dukes, et cetera, I feel honoured by your presence here today to accept the hospitality of a British farmer and hunt a Cotswold hare. When I first saw you

HRH Prince Charles of Bourbon

French gentlefolks riding over the wall bang in front of a well-mounted field I was told you were frog eaters. Never, I said. Never. No French chaps could sit down and ride like that to hounds. I have been converted from the error of my ways. Now I'm prepared to back you on horseback against any Englishman over the Cotswold walls. My noble guests, I sincerely trust that that fellow Napoleon won't abdicate just yet. Why? 'Cos we should lose you and it will be a bad day for us all. May we forever see your horses' footmarks on our land. We are proud of our Royal exiles, for we have learnt to respect and honour the brave and true sons of France.'

He then turned to his son Tom and bade him bring the biggest of the silver cups he had won at steeplechasing on the Cotswolds and filled it to the brim with champagne.

'Now,' said Charles, handing the great two-handled goblet to the duke, 'please oblige me by drinking out of my son's winnings in your own country's wine. Then we will have a little hollering.' One can only imagine what Charles Cook meant by that.

The Duc d'Orléans

Although the Duc d'Aumarle came to live at Wood Norton in 1857, several years before he actually bought it, and lived there until 1871 when he was permitted to return to France, he must have felt somewhat insecure because the following year he purchased Wood Norton Estate, to which he returned for a while when he was again banished from France in 1886. The estate eventually comprised several villages in the vale and the Cotswolds, 4,000 acres for £200,000. The duke died in 1897 and the whole of the estate became the property of his great-nephew, the Duc d'Orléans.

The Duc d'Orléans came to live at Wood Norton after rebuilding the mansion in 1898 and was joined by his wife and sister, Princess Louise Françoise. He lived in his new mansion in some regal splendour, with liveried footmen and many servants, and enjoyed life to the full. He was a skilful sportsman, an excellent shot and golfer, and a keen motorist, driving himself in a Renault.

Wood Norton Hall became the last word in nineteenth-century extravagance. The duchess was very definite in her ideas of

74

decoration. There were fleur de lis motifs over every window and door. The duke's marble bath had steps down into it. It was all very grand and I was very impressed. One could write volumes about the zoo he created with animals brought back from his expeditions abroad. (This zoo was seen by two old friends of mine, Mr Gill Smith and Mr Alf Baker.) When the duke returned from one of his Arctic tours polar bears were brought in trucks to Evesham railway station and a bear pit built in the hall grounds. Kangaroos hopped among the blackberry bushes. Kings and queens, abdicated and ruling, came for the pheasant shoots in the woods.

In 1904 the duke invited his elder sister and her husband to stay. The king, Carlos, was a great shot, and a thousand pheasants were bagged one day. Alf Tidmarsh, our shepherd, was working on the estate and was one of the beaters at the pheasant shoot. He saw three pheasants falling in the air at the same time from the King of Portugal's gun. The birds flew high between the trees, but the king's loader was smart on the job.

The end of a day's shoot

Wood Norton Hall

The building of the mansion and the life style of the duke brought great prosperity to Evesham at the turn of the century. Lowes advertised themselves as 'Drapers to His Royal Highness the Duke of Orléans'. It seemed that the Evesham trades people were not backward in their advertising.

My mother worked at Lowes as a girl, making ball gowns for the royal family and shaping and putting together riding habits for the ladies who rode side-saddle. She told me of a gown she helped to make for the Duchesse de Guise and the fitting of it – quite something for a nineteen-year-old girl to remember. Arthur Wheatley went one better than Lowes the Drapers, describing himself as 'Anatomical Bootmaker' and 'Bootmaker by appointment to the Duke of Orléans'. His plaque still stands today in High Street, Evesham.

The Wheatleys were great musicians and one member of the family was christened Handel Wheatley. When King Carlos of Portugal came to Wood Norton Hall in 1904 at least two Evesham babies were christened Carlos in his honour. Such was the effect of the royal exiles. Evesham was lifted from something ordinary to something special.

Ben Wasley, the duke's head gamekeeper, rode a horse the mile and a half to Evesham every day and shopped for a few odds and ends for the royal family. He rode with two panniers across the horse's back to carry the groceries. One day the duke decided to do the shopping himself. However, outside a pub known as the Jolly Gardeners the horse stopped and refused to budge. Out came the landlord with a pint of ale and a lump of sugar for the horse. Although he expected to see Wasley, as usual, he was quite unperturbed and gave the pint to his royal guest and the sugar to the horse.

One of the show-pieces of Wood Norton Hall are the Golden Gates, said to be a replica of the gates of the Royal Palace of Versailles, restored to perfection by a local blacksmith in 1977. Soon after they were installed in the autumn of 1907 it became

The golden gates at Wood Norton

known that Princess Louise Françoise, youngest daughter of the late Compte de Paris and a sister of the duke, was to marry Prince Charles of Bourbon Sicily at Wood Norton. It would be the first royal wedding in Worcestershire for six hundred years. Lord Coventry asked the gentlemen of Worcestershire to subscribe a maximum of two guineas each towards a wedding gift for the royal couple of some Worcester china.

The duke felt compelled to build a new chapel on his estate for the ceremony and imported twenty-five bandsmen from France to play in it. It was built in a Roman style with a great vaulted roof supported by stone pilasters, cloisters joined the chapel to the big house, and the stone blocks were all carved with the fleur de lis. He also had a marquee erected for the grand reception, the canopy painted in an antique style. This was in addition to the 80 x 40 foot banqueting hall, decorated in a grand fashion.

As the special trains drew into Evesham station the townsfolk saw the glitter of the fabulous uniform worn by the King of Spain and the lace, diamonds and pearls which adorned his queen. The Queen of Portugal and the Duc de Guise came in a dining car from Folkestone. There were ambassadors from Spain, Russia, Austria, Belgium, Denmark, Norway, Greece, Romania, Serbia and the USA. All the people were met personally by the duke and duchess, who put fifty cars at their disposal. The chauffeurs who brought the guests from London returned the next day. Some Evesham residents took advantage of a free ride and went in the cars to the capital. It was quite an event in 1907.

On 16 November the Roman Catholic Archbishop of Birmingham was to marry the royal bride and groom in the gorgeous chapel. Then came the problem – the chapel was not registered for weddings. And a Roman Catholic wedding could not be held in Worcester Cathedral either.

Now there were plans to one day build a Roman Catholic church in Evesham High Street. In fact, it was not built until about 1910 and the Catholics meanwhile worshipped in a tin tabernacle

Prince Charles and his bride

The Catholic church at Evesham, the site of the royal wedding

on the building site. The royal wedding had to take place in that tabernacle, built in corrugated iron and painted in lead paint. What a disappointment for the duke who had designed the chapel at the hall with such care and with such taste. He tried hard to keep the new arrangement quiet in the town but it did leak out. Just close relatives attended the civil ceremony, but on that wedding morning Evesham High Street was packed with sightseers. The guests then retired to the chapel and banqueting hall at Wood Norton.

The wedding cost the duke £80,000, a bill from which he never recovered. The bear pits were closed, the giraffes died. The duke shot the deer and sold the venison in London. Some was sent abroad. The duchess was no mean marksman with a rifle and she shot young bucks and does like a sniper.

Memories of the wedding ceremony in the red-oxide painted iron tabernacle rankled. What would the duke have thought had he lived to see the grandson of that married couple become King Juan Carlos, the restored King of Spain.

In 1912 the estate was sold and after leaving Wood Norton the duke travelled extensively in the Arctic and the African continent, frequently staying at the homes of various members of the Bourbon family in Spain and Italy until his death in 1926. There is no doubt that from 1857 until 1912 the town of Evesham benefited no end from the exiled royal family. After their departure the estate of 4,000 acres and large portions of the parishes of Fladbury, Bishampton, Harventon and Church Lench were split up.

As with any folk in the public eye, especially royalty, rumours were prevalent about their life-style. One rumour I heard was that parties of beautiful French girls came to Evesham railway station to stay at Wood Norton Hall for the French families there and for their pleasure. These beautiful girls, it was said, were replaced periodically by more. It is hearsay, as are other stories of drunken orgies at the hall, when furniture was burnt at night on the terrace. One servant, who served the royal family, said that he learnt all his bad habits while at Wood Norton!

The Duc d'Orléans in his Renault car

CHAPTER TWELVE

HORSEMEN AND
COW DOCTORS

Earlier in this century vets were only called upon in serious cases, when animals could not be treated or cured by the cow doctor, and there were four men who lived under the shadow of Bredon Hill who were both horsemen and cow doctors. Jimmy Pardington, Percy Nind, Tom Baldwyn, affectionately known as Laughing Tom, and Bob Sinderberry all shared their experiences with me. These were gifted men in their own right, who knew from their experience whether livestock thrived or not.

JIMMY PARDINGTON

If I had never met Jimmy Pardington something would have been missing from my life. Without a doubt Jimmy was to me as much a part of the Bredon Hill scene as the row of fir trees above Grafton where he hacked around those walled-in fields and the quarry. He was then bailiff for Captain Case of Beckford Hall, having just finished his stint of soldiering in the Middle East at the end of the First World War. He was a man who lived for horses; he understood them and it seemed they understood him. He broke them in with kindness.

He was quite a slim, shortish man who wore moleskin trousers, a bush shirt and a semi-cowboy trilby which always intrigued me. His walk made no secret of the fact that Jimmy had spent long hours in the saddle.

Horses were not his sole interest, however, and as a bailiff he did his own shepherding on the hill, and kept a dairy herd for the hall, producing butter and cream in plenty.

His years as bailiff were remarkable in many other ways too. He told me how the stooks of wheat were so close together in one field that the carter could not get the wagon through the gate to pick up the sheaves until they carried some through the gateway. Jimmy was a bit of a romancer, I knew, but his prowess as a grower of mangel wurzels was unequalled. For years he won the cup for growing the heaviest yield per acre; 60 tons was his record.

In his large garden at Beckford Hall Jimmy grew dahlias to perfection, winning prizes at the flower shows of the Midlands and further afield. He showed me the secret of his success. He had a cider barrel of water where he put the soiled clippings, or beltings, from the sheep on the hill together with household soot. The liquid manure fed his dahlias. Mind you, I reckon he learnt a wrinkle or two from father-in-law Fred Davis, who grew such splendid blooms of begonias and dahlias. In Jimmy's greenhouse leaves of homegrown tobacco were dried and cured. I don't know how he cured the leaves but I gather that a dressing of rum was included. To sit with Jimmy in his living-room was an experience indeed. The smoke from his pipe didn't smell like the known brands of tobacco! I've always enjoyed the smell of a garden fire with plenty of couch grass dormering away on a winter's evening. Jimmy's tobacco smelt not unlike that, but it did involve the use of lots of matches.

Jimmy was fortunate to get the post as Captain Case's bailiff but he was a likeable fellow who had hunted with the Croome Hounds under Major Gresson, their Master. When the war came, Jimmy volunteered for the Yeomanry and soon was promoted to Farrier Sergeant. Out in Salonica the major recognized Jimmy on a parade.

'Pardington,' he shouted, 'What are you doing in the ranks? A man of your ability and skill with horses should be an officer.'

Jimmy was promoted in the field, becoming a Second Lieutenant almost overnight.

He once told me of his equestrian experiences in the army. He was a man devoted to the care of animals and was disgusted by the way the Turks, the enemy at the time, treated their horses so cruelly. When Jimmy and his fellow officers were not in action they held horse races in the desert. He noticed that the first horse away kicked up such a screen of sand that it was almost impossible for the rest of the field to see and keep to the course. He soon realized how he could take advantage of this and by setting the pace on his horse won a small trophy.

High on Bredon Hill before Jimmy was born, Stephen and Violetta Davis were farming St Catherine's Farm, Woollas Hill. They had two children, Fred and Violetta. In 1879 Fred married and his parents moved out of the farm. Fred's bride, Emma Milward, brought a dowry of £40,000 with her, enabling Fred to follow the sort of life he had hankered for – that of a racehorse trainer. He became very successful using the limestone plateau of Bredon Hill for training and operating a small racecourse up there. Jimmy Pardington met Fred's daughter on that hill. They began their courting on that hill, and eventually got married.

In the 1920s Jimmy Pardington used to take surplus fruit to Pershore Market. His gamekeeper, Joe Whittle, rode one of his hunters over the hill. One day a chap from one of the hill villages drove into the market with a load of plums. Jimmy, with his usual flair for picking a winner, stopped the man and said, 'When you have unloaded your dray I'd like a word with you. Do you want to sell that horse, Governor? Because I'd like to buy him.'

'Well,' the man replied, 'I would sell at a price. Fifty quid.'

Jimmy didn't answer for a minute but when he did the reply was, 'Forty-five pounds'. And he bought it for forty-five guineas. He told me it was the best horse he ever rode. His purchase had been little short of ingenious.

That winter Jimmy hunted the horse with the Croome Hounds. He also entered it for an amateur riders race at Cheltenham and won the cup. He named the horse KBO or 'Keep Buggering On'.

In his eighties Jimmy still used to drive his old Morris car into town. He had his own ideas about motoring, telling me that every car should have a starting handle – useful, he said, on cold mornings.

Going to town this old Morris took up a bit more than half of the road. The smoke from Jimmy's big cherry pipe wafted from the open window like a couch grass fire. Lorry drivers trying to pass shouted at him, but Jimmy just waved back saying, 'Ah, someone else knows me.'

In the High Street, before the days of traffic wardens, the car was abandoned rather than parked. His driving was not exactly dangerous, just a hindrance to others whose lives progressed at a greater pace.

PERCY NIND

Percy Nind was a contemporary of Jimmy Pardington, living in the same village, but born with a silver spoon in his mouth. His mother was a Baldwyn and his father a prosperous farmer. Thoroughly spoiled by his mother as a young man Percy, after his father's death, farmed as a gentleman farmer, very smartly dressed, always astride a useful hunter. During the First World War Percy made a bit of money buying horses for the War Effort from neighbouring farms. An astute judge of horse flesh he was a regular buyer at the Cheltenham Repository. Carters in Gloucestershire hated to see Percy around, knowing that he was bent on buying the very best horses from farmers. Some hid their best animals in loose boxes.

As a cow doctor Percy was quite an expert, but his skill at castrating animals was well known in the vale and on the hills. A man who would do anything but farm in the conventional way, Percy was happy to leave the running of his land to a couple of old men while he spent his time wheeling and dealing. The fact was that at that time Percy was pretty well breeched, not short of a few bob.

Percy, as I knew him, was a tall upright man dressed in moleskin trousers, a sleeved waistcoat and brown boots. This was when he was pottering around his farm or at our place castrating calves. On hunting day Percy was one of the most handsome of followers of the Croome Hounds, sitting on his horse at the Meet chatting up the ladies, drinking his Stirrup Cup, pandering to the Master. He knew Bredon Hill like the back of his hand. Other riders would tire their horses out riding up and down the steep gradient after the hounds as the fox went from one coppice to another. Percy sat astride his horse on the flat of the hill where he watched the hounds until they returned. The fox was not the only creature that went into those coppices. Percy and one of his ladies tied their hunters to the coppice fence and among the beech trees Percy entertained his partner. We won't speculate as to what took place. Percy did tell me that there were more bones made on Bredon Hill than were broken on hunting days! The hunting horn often sounded 'gone to ground'. Percy and his partner had also gone to ground!

However, everything fell apart for Percy when his mother died. It was sad to see how he let himself go. He had been a womanizer but unfortunately never married. Gradually Percy's life style altered from the smart young man whose mother had looked after him so well, even idolizing him, to an untidy fellow. He never got up until midday, then, unshaven and unwashed, he went to the Working Men's Club in the evening. He still had some of his former self but his house became a dump. I visited him quite often and seeing a pile of tobacco tins on the large table in the dining room asked him why they were there.

'I never like throwing anything away,' he replied.

In the garden a miniature mangel bury of tins heaped up along the fence. I liked old Percy, despite his failings, and he still retained

Bait time on the binder

something of the aristocracy of the Baldwyns. He still took the money at village dances and when a chap from the next village went to one, Percy said in his quaint way, 'What are you doing down here then? Because I have always said that if we can't find a fox in Ashton Wood, you won't find one in Beckford Coppice.'

Percy lived at the end of Rabbit Lane in Beckford. When I visited him he always followed me to my car. There was no way that I could shake him off as he related one story after another about the ladies of the hunt.

The last time I saw Percy at his farmhouse he was sitting by the fire warming some cider in a saucepan. He had got a flu cold and I told him I'd get the doctor to him.

'No,' he replied. 'If you fetch the doctor he will have me in hospital and this place will get cold and damp.'

It was cold and damp and Percy did spend his last months in hospital.

Up in his bedroom the sash window was permanently open. A branch from the ash tree in the garden had grown through the window into the room. When I remarked on this fact to Percy he laughed and replied, 'That branch comes in very useful. I knock my pipe out on it every night before I get into bed.'

Percy was a character and he enjoyed his life – not a wasted life, but he was certainly not a nine till five man.

TOM BALDWYN

Tom Baldwyn was the last of a line of gentlemen farmers in the village. It's true he didn't retain the life style of his ancestors but the aristocratic presence was there. He was in his seventies during the war when he came to see me. I had 11 acres of oats fit to carry on the slope of Bredon Hill.

'Do you want a hand harvesting the oats?' he said.

I was pleased with the offer and he promised to be along after he had milked his house cow in the morning.

He came about eight o'clock, bringing his own shuppick (pitchfork). I loaded the wagons with Roy, a boy of sixteen. Mr Baldwyn pitched the sheaves with another Tom, my cowman. What a handy man he was, this old farmer.

When the oat rick was three-quarters finished Tom said, 'Frederick, have you got a harrow around?'

I replied, 'Yes, there's a set of harrows under the hedge.'

Tom Whittle, the cowman, was building the rick and had started to put the roof on. Mr Baldwyn took the harrow up the ladder and

Harvesting the oats

fixed it on the side of the roof. I was on the wagon unloading the sheaves. Mr Baldwyn then dug his hobnailed boot heel first in between the tines of the harrow and faced me.

'Now then, let's have 'em.' He spoke these words with his eternal laugh, a happy man known affectionately as Laughing Tom. I tossed the first sheaf to him and he caught it on his fork, pitching it to Roy and Tom on the rick. This man was so ambidextrous that he could toss the sheaves either side of him. We had never seen his like before.

After four days the harvesting was finished. I went to his little farm, The Croft, to thank him and pay him. He had retired from farming but still kept his house cow for milk, and Old English game fowls.

'Come on in and have a drop of cider,' was his invitation.

'No thanks, Mr Baldwyn, I don't drink cider.'

His cider was quite famous in the vale. An Evesham gentleman I knew said it made him feel benevolent. It had different affects on some of the locals, who could get in a fighting mood.

I sat down in his kitchen over a cup of tea. His sister came in with a cake. She had been making butter. On the ceiling racks there were great flitches of bacon, fat and mature. He talked to me of days gone by when the squire farmed most of the land. He told me how when the squire's cows caught foot and mouth disease they kept them alive with sloppy bran mashes. They couldn't eat and they went thin but they stayed alive.

'Now,' I said. 'How much do I owe you?'

He gave me what appeared to be a fatherly look, cleared his throat and said, 'There's a war on. I didn't come for money, I did the work for the good of the cause.'

No man who worked for me had ever spoken like that before and I was nonplussed.

'That's good of you, Mr Baldwyn, to think like that but I must pay you. You worked for four days.'

I'd said my piece and was about to pay him when he had the last word.

''Twas only three days.'

I paid him for three days.

At Christmas he came to kill my pig, bringing all the tools of the trade – steel yard balances, hooks, ropes, knives, steels. He was pretty adept at pig killing.

When it came to cutting up the carcase the following day he said, 'How do you want me to cut him up?'

When I replied, 'Use your own discretion,' he laughed.

'Discretion be damned. There's as many ways of cutting up a pig as there are pigs.'

I left it to him but every bone he came to had a name. The backbone he called the Lazarus.

'Do you want any chines?' he questioned when he was about to cut up Lazarus. 'They always keeps the chines salted for a christening. Any signs of a christening?' he laughed, for he knew I'd only recently got married.

Mr Baldwyn's experience with animals was valued in the village for he could be called a cow doctor, or amateur vet. In those days before antibiotics and cortisone Tom Baldwyn's remedy for 'foul in the foot', a common complaint in cows, worked. The foot was put into a stocking made from a small sack, and the stocking filled with hot bran and salt to draw out the infection.

To give a cow which had lost its cud a drench of boiling fat bacon in cabbage water seems repulsive, but, as Mr Baldwyn said, 'It's a cure'. But he kept a valuable instrument in his cow shed, which we borrowed more than once. It's called a probang, a pipe which would bend and it was about 3 feet long and 1 inch in diameter with a lead weight at the end. This probang was used to dislodge a stoppage in a cow's gullet, such as a potato or a piece of mangel. By thrusting the tube down the gullet it would relieve the stoppage, saving the cow's life. In those days we treated husk, a distressing cough in young cattle, by dribbling a tablespoonful of mixture up each nostril to kill the grub in the windpipe, the mixture being spirit of hartshorn, turpentine and linseed oil. It made the animal's eyes water but it cured the husk. I did learn quite a lot about the treatment of animals from Tom Baldwyn. I wish that some more of his ways could be recalled.

BOB SINDERBERRY

Another amateur vet who should be remembered is Bob Sinderberry. He farmed News Farm, Ashton under Hill, with one of the finest teams of horses I've ever seen. He had a knack of treating what was known among the horse copers (dealers) in those days as left-handed 'uns or screws.

He bought a screw, a trap horse which was nothing but skin and bone, for £10 in Gloucester Market. He soon had it fit and well; it was a treat to see this animal pulling his trap up the village street. It

A carter and his horses

picked up its legs and Bob sat back as the trap rocked from side to side at a pace.

This man had some skills he had inherited from the gypsies. He carried something in his pocket which attracted any horse difficult to catch. Bob could put a halter on and the horses came to him, but his method was a secret which he never divulged.

Bob kept a white Shorthorn bull to cover his red Shorthorn cows, thus getting roan calves. He personally fed the cart-horses in his stable damping the bait (chaff, mangolds, oat flour) with the urine from his slop pail. What that did for them I don't know. They always looked sleek and they were what we called prompt.

Bob's son Tom worshipped the horses and he ploughed the Worcestershire clay with a four-horse team, but times were changing with the war and more land had to be ploughed. Bob bought a Fordson tractor and Tom learnt to drive it. He had been ploughing all day in a big field called Cinder Meadow. At tea-time Bob met him in the yard with these words, 'Tom, that ploughing is going well I see, so after tea do another couple of hours now the weather's fine.'

Tom's reply is a classic, the typical thoughts of a horse man.

'But Father, that tractor has done her shot for today. I'm not going to maul her by working with her after tea.'

CHAPTER THIRTEEN

PIONEERS AMONG THE MARKET GARDENERS

One thing that fascinates me is the way that varieties of fruit, vegetables and flowers have evolved; I once grew 11 acres of plums with about twenty different varieties. So many names of fruit are just a memory, they have become extinct, and others can be classified as rare breeds.

Either side of the village street varieties of pears grew along the hedgerow. Names like Hessle, Windsor, Beurre de Clairgow, Clapps Favourite, Louis Bonne and the little Burgundy pear with such a delicate flavour come to mind. What we see in the shops today are Conference and Commice, very choice fruit but the old varieties did have their individual flavour.

So many of our apples have disappeared from the shops. Cox's Orange remains supreme as a dessert apple, while the Bramley Seedling is unbeatable for cooking and keeping. Absent but remembered are cookers like Warners King, known as Drunken Willy, Lord Derby, Ecklinville, Gascoines Scarlet and Normanton.

Plums in the shops are mainly Victorias, a lovely dessert plum, Czar, a cooker, Greengage, for dessert, Pershore Egg plum, another cooker, Early Prolific, dual purpose, and Marjorie Seedling, a late plum for dessert. It seems that we have retained a number of good varieties of plums but some we don't see much today are the Heron, a good early dessert fruit, Jimmy Moore, a rival to Victorias, Orleans, with a very good flavour, Golden Drop, a greengage type of fruit, and Warwickshire Drooper, a late dual purpose plum.

Walter Martin, who lived from 1828 until 1919, raised a plum known as Martin's Seedling, or Purple Pershore. On one of the Manor Cottages called No Gains, in Pershore, where he lived, a Blue Diamond grew. The flower of this tree was pollinated by Martin with pollen from River's Early Prolific plums. He sowed the seed obtained in a flowerpot. In 1877 he moved to Drakes Broughton 3 miles from Pershore, where he rented 10 acres of woodland which he gradually grubbed. Here he planted his little tree, took grafts from it and grafted it on suckers. He cultivated his holding until 1900, and like many benefactors of the human race, though he did not become rich, he was a happy and contented man. In March 1919, when he was ninety-one years old, he was busy digging up plum suckers on the day before his death.

Walter's contribution to plum growing in the Vale of Evesham may sound trivial, he introduced just one variety, but it was a variety which proved to be one of the best plums for canning. Many thousands of trees grew from the seeds of that little tree grown at No Gains. When Martin's Seedling, or Purple Pershore, was ripe it could be eaten as a dessert fruit. It was a bit what we call tart, but for bottling or canning it was supreme. During the war, when prunes were unavailable, experiments were made to manufacture prunes from our plums. The variety experimented with was Martin's Purple Pershore. This plum, despite its name, is no relation to the Pershore Egg plum, a yellow cooking plum which makes the finest jam.

The Pershore Egg plum was discovered by another Pershore man named Mr Crooke. It's said he found it growing wild in Tydesley Wood a few miles from Pershore. It's been grown since early in the last century. Most plums have to be grafted on to stocks but the Pershore Egg plum grows from the sucker it produces and is a good stock to graft other varieties on to.

Spires Bros were nurserymen in Worcester Road, Evesham. In the 1920s they grew all varieties of plums, selling the young trees to the fruit growers of the vale. One Pershore Egg plum tree which grew against a shed in their nursery grew red plums on just one of its branches, the rest being the usual yellow. I saw this tree when on a visit to the nursery with Dad. The fruit and the branch were called a sport or a freak but Spires Bros saw it as a rival to the Victoria, being red and egg-shaped. Grafts were taken from that branch and grafted on to suckers until there were enough to sell to the fruit growers. The new variety was called Evesham Wonder. After a few years Dad and his partner bought fifty young trees from the nursery at 7s 6d each. It's a well-known fact that the public will buy red plums in preference to yellow ones but this red plum tasted exactly like the yellow plum, its parent, and the Evesham Wonder never took on.

During the war my brother grew tons of plums for processing. He picked his yellow egg plums when they were green. That's how the factory preferred them. Having some Evesham Wonder trees his men picked them green and they went with the Pershore Egg plums. The trouble was, although they were green they came out red in the cans when they were processed.

In the community of market gardeners and farmers in the Vale of Evesham there has always been a race, a contest, between growers to get their crop to market before their neighbour. Wallflowers were noticed when they bloomed in February, the plants were marked and the resulting seed saved and jealously guarded.

In the early days of sprout growing it was usual to plant the seed in sheltered gardens in February and transplant the seedlings in May. Mr George Bury, who farmed at Netherton near Elmley Castle, used to plant his sprout seed with a corn drill and sell sprout plants. One year when he drilled his winter wheat at Elm Farm in September, a little sprout seed had been left in the corn drill. Walking in his wheat field in the spring he noticed a few sprout plants growing among the young wheat. The plants had survived the winter so he pulled them up and planted them on a part of one of his fields and grew a very early crop of sprouts. It was George Bury who first grew autumn-sown sprout plants by chance. Scores of growers followed, planting in the autumn to catch the early market.

Webbs of Mickleton had greenhouses where they grew tomatoes. They were the first to grow early sprout plants under glass. It's surprising how sprouts marketed in August will sell when lots of other vegetables are available. I like to think of George Bury as the pioneer in growing early sprouts. There's quite a famous tune played by brass bands called 'Watching the Wheat'. It was lucky for George Bury that he watched his wheat!

Auction markets have always intrigued me. Auctioneers in particular are a race apart. The good ones are better entertainers than those we hear or see on radio or television. The produce of the Vale of Evesham, whether the plums developed by Walter Martin or George Bury's sprouts, were sold by auction in local markets. It seems that the heyday of fruit and vegetable auctions occurred between the two world wars. Now more is sold by private dealing.

The central market at Evesham was where I sold my fruit and vegetables. This market was started by two brothers, Fred and Ernest Beck, at the turn of the century. The chief sales were on Mondays, Wednesdays and Thursdays. When I first started taking produce there the auctioneer was Mr Albert Lavell. He was a great character with a wonderful head for figures, possibly the fastest auctioneer in his day. The bays in the market would be full of asparagus, plums, etc., in their season. One memorable day in August the whole market was full of Victoria plums, all sold by Albert Lavell.

Before the sale began the auctioneer, talking to the merchants and on the phone to city markets, got an idea how the trade would be that day. His clerk had to be quick at reckoning and booking, for when the trade was good Mr Lavell sold as quickly as he could walk. This man, who was a genius at selling runner beans, would start business by saying, 'Now gentlemen, how much these chips of runners?' (The beans were in chips of 8 pounds each.) 'Fourpence

George Hunting, sprout-picking champion, with Tom Archer and Mr Cartwright

did I hear? Four and a half, Charles Barnett.' He walked along the line of beans saying, 'Four and a half' until someone said, 'five'.

When he reached a stack of very choice stick beans the merchants would compete for these.

'Five and a half.'

'Six.'

'Six and a half.'

This might not seem like an ordinary auction but the growers, the merchants and the auctioneer knew the trade of the day and Albert Lavell had a lot of produce to move.

I remember taking beans to the market one Wednesday and they made 6*d* a pound. I took another fifty chips in on Thursday and the market was full of beans. Mr Lavell sold the first few chips at 3*d* a pound, then there was no offer for the rest. A glut of beans had become a reality in the Midlands, and my beans were unsold. Geoff, a well-known vegetable merchant and a member of

Bengeworth church choir with a rich baritone voice, sang to all of us in the market that day. 'The Strife is o'er, the Battle won. Hallelujah'. Very apt, I thought, except that the battle had not been won by anybody. I loaded my pick-up with my unsold beans and took some to the hospital, others to friends, rather than them being dumped at the Council tip. Next day before the sale Mr Lavell said, adding insult to injury, 'When so many beans were unsold someone stole fifty chips from the market.'

I told him that I had picked up my fifty chips of beans which were unsold. He laughed and said, 'Well done, but you know someone came here in the afternoon and paid one penny a pound for all the beans in the market, but there were fifty chips short.'

The market in those days was an education. The merchants did try to get the better of the auctioneer at times, but he kept them in order. Like children they threw sprouts and plums at each other, and fixed labels under the collar of other merchants. The humour was quite elementary.

A grower named Tommy Nightingale said to me one day, 'I'm not putting my sprouts in nets made in Hong Kong in Communist China. I'm going to see Bert Lavell about buying nets from Communist China.'

I said, 'Hong Kong isn't in Communist China, Tommy.'

He replied, 'Un't it? I allus thought it was.'

Another grower asked one of Mr Lavell's clerks how the parsnip trade was. His words were, 'How was the snip trade yesterday?'

The clerk, who suffered from what is commonly called affectation, replied, 'There is definitely an upward trend, parsnips are more readily in demand.'

The grower was flabbergasted and Mr Lavell came into the office.

'What's the trouble, George?'

George replied, 'I asked your clerk how the snip trade was yesterday and he came out with something about trends.'

Mr Lavell looked up the prices on the sale sheets for the previous day and told George what parsnips were making.

So here, in Albert Lavell, we have something of an entrepreneur, a man with a Council school education who had become a craftsman at his profession as an auctioneer. His father was an engine driver on the railway; his aunt went to school with Mother.

Albert became a Christian Scientist and was in demand lecturing on that subject. He made several trips to America on lecture tours. His new life style seemed to suit him, a very generous man who learnt to play the organ and became a great exponent on that instrument. Many's the time, after a hectic day in the office and the sale ring, when Albert cooled off on the organ at All Saints or in his own rather grand house on Green Hill. He was always immaculately dressed and had his own initials, A.E.L., on his Jaguar car. His new status never went to his head though and the number of struggling small market gardeners he has helped will never be known.

One Saturday evening I was at the hairdressers and Albert was having his hair cut. An old Evesham market gardener came into the saloon. They spoke to each other, then this man began his reminiscence.

'I remember thee, Bert, when thee was at school with the ass out of your trousers. Your father was an engine driver on the Midland Railway. You lived in a little old cottage by the Gas Works.'

Bert replied, 'That's perfectly true, George, what you say, times were hard. Dad did drive a railway engine.' He continued, 'I remember you, George. You and your dad had 10 acres of ground and a horse and dray in those days. Let me see, you still have 10 acres of ground and a horse and dray.'

No more was said but it seemed that George had not used his talents, if he had any. I think of Albert Lavell as a typical self-made man, climbing from office boy to managing director. It's good that he broke the mould. Must a man like forever the same things, must his interests always be fixed?

When Bert Lavell was running the central market, produce flooded in from all parts of the Vale of Evesham. The growers knew that they would get the current price when Mr Lavell was auctioneer. From the time when the plum trees were in blow (I like that Shakespearian phrase) until picking time the growers watched their plums develop. Victoria plums too thick on the branches were small and useless, and a late frost could spell ruin to the growers. It's a sad story when men who depended on their plum crop were denied an income because of the spring frost.

The Midland folk who came in their cars on Blossom Sunday touring Pershore and the Lenches knew little of the anxiety suffered by the growers. The picture was a varied one in the 1920s. After losing a crop some growers drank themselves silly in their hovels and did no work for a week. It was said that there were suicides among the growers because of their losses. Maybe it happened. I knew of one case, but the little master men who cared for their land were a philosophical lot. One man I knew, when the frost struck his fruit, replied to the parson who went to console him, 'Oh, the birds fed Elishah. We will survive, there's always next year.'

CHAPTER FOURTEEN

THREE BAKERS

Some years ago in the village we had the choice of three bakers. Hugh Clements was the village baker, Percy Smith came with his horse and cart from Beckford delivering bread and Careful Billy delivered twice a week from that village with a covered wagon which reminded me of the advert for Atora Beef Suet.

Hugh Clements was a countryman extraordinaire. When I first knew him he kept the village post office. The post was delivered from Tewkesbury every morning by a horse and mail cart driven by Charlie Booth. The postman could be relied upon, and his horse would be trotting up the village street every morning at 8 o'clock. He stabled his horse in Hugh Clements' stable next to his cow shed. Hugh Clements then delivered the letters. Winter and summer Charlie Booth worked, doing the gardens of the village folk until about 4 o'clock. Then he took the mail back to Tewkesbury.

Hugh Clements was an ambitious man and had his finger in lots of pies. The fact was that Mrs Clements, his wife, was an extremely good business woman. An excellent baker, Hugh also ran a flock of sheep, kept poultry and had a small herd of Shorthorn cows. His family delivered milk in the village. There was a little competition from The Midnight Milkman, but he was not very reliable. Hugh's dairy, near the bakehouse, had a very polished brass or copper churn on wheels which was used for delivering the half pints, pints and quarts around the village.

On Saturdays Hugh could be seen in the Wynch Field as Secretary of the Football Club in winter and scorer of the Cricket

Club in summer. He was also churchwarden at St Barbara's church. So Hugh was as much part of the village scene as the slope up Bredon Hill. His land went up those slopes to the Cuckoo Pen where he grazed his sheep. His milking cows ran in the brook-side meadows.

I visited the bakehouse sometimes to collect a dough cake, something he had a knack of making, and so moreish. I watched Hugh take the loaves from the oven with his peel, a shovel-like implement. The smell lingers of his delicious dough cakes and milk loaves. In those days he cooked the Sunday joints in his oven for lots of the village folk.

But there was much more to this baker, dairyman, postman, farmer than was apparent to many folk: it was his personality. He was a jolly man, always with a smile, and a useful shot with his twelve-bore gun. He was a man who entertained the football team on the hill around Holcombe Knapp for a day's rabbiting, then provided a slap-up meal with plenty of cider at the bakehouse.

On one of these occasions Hugh lost his favourite ferret in a rabbit warren near The Cuckoo Pen. Now Hugh was an emotional man, who felt the loss very much. At the meal afterwards he shed a few tears over the ferret, then he sang 'Tomorrow the sun may be shining although it is cloudy today'. I liked Hugh's attitude to life.

At the village concerts I thought Mr Clements was a star turn. His inimitable style of singing, he had a gentle tenor voice, and the unending repertoire of his old songs always fascinated me as a small boy. Lots of his songs went with him when he died. They remain unsung today, although I still recall some. I have one regret, that about a month before he died it was arranged for Hugh to tape-record his collection of folk songs, but it was never done.

Here's one I remember from the village concerts:

John Jones he had a party on Tuesday of last week.
George Biggs was there as usual with all his sauce and cheek.
He said 'You chaps, I just have pinched a sovereign from a pal,

Shall we have smokes and drinks with it?'
I said 'Of course we shall.'
We had brandies round and ninepenny smokes
We quite enjoyed the spree.
We sang, we roared, we chuckled aloud with glee.
We screamed and howled
And thought the joke was fine.
I didn't know till afterwards
The quid he pinched was mine.

After two years of marriage my wife gave birth to a daughter. Meeting Mr Clements in the street he said to me, 'Well, Fred. You have proved yourself a man.'

I said, 'Thank you', and realized that to be the father of a daughter was supposed to prove just that.

Hugh Clements, like many farmers at that time, used to take his lambs to market on a dray with racks around. His fast-trotting horse was known as Express. One winter's day our shepherd Tidmarsh came to our door in quite a sweat. I should explain that apart from having Hugh Clements as a neighbour on one side we had Mr William Hughes on the other side. That day all the ewes in three flocks got mixed up. Alf Tidmarsh described it saying, 'Your ewes are with Hugh's ewes and Hughes's ewes are with your ewes. There's a Western Horn Tup with them that stinks like a billy goat [Mr William Hughes's].'

The rams got fighting that day too and Hugh Clements' ram was killed and he had to be compensated.

As the village grew between the wars, more folk began tapping the water supply from Paris on the Hill. The problem was that houses at the top of the village were almost as high up as the reservoir at Paris. The Council got worried about this. At a parish meeting I attended one villager after another said that the main supply should not be tapped by anyone else because of this limited supply. Hugh Clements told us of the quantity of water the springs yielded and of Mrs Church, who lived in the highest house in the village on the water main. He said, 'The supply is better than you realize. Mrs Church's house is the highest point in the village. The water gets up into her bedroom. I know because I've been there.'

'Oh, Mr Clements!' Mrs Church gasped.

There was nothing amiss. Mr Church, the dentist, was ill for years, and Hugh was a regular visitor.

From their school-days Hugh Clements and my father were great friends. He was a man whose experience and opinion could be relied upon and I doubt we will ever see his like again.

We didn't have bread from Hugh Clements very often as for some years Dad had dealt with Percy Smith, as his mother had done. Percy Smith, the Beckford baker, delivered bread three times a week to Ashton under Hill. The family business had been going for generations.

Percy had been a very early member of the Boy Scouts movement. He and Harry Baker, a relative and a neighbour, were among the Beckford troop who camped at Elmley Park, General Davies' Estate, before the First World War. I believe it was 1910 when that camp occurred. Baden-Powell, who became Lord Baden-Powell, and General Roberts visited that camp and rode horseback up Ashton village street. They had a bread and cheese lunch at The White Hart at Ashton kept by Samuel Cope.

Percy Smith and Harry Baker joined the Army in 1914. On Easter Sunday the following year many of their battalion were killed in Mesopotamia.

Like Hugh Clements, Percy Smith was a parish councillor, a stalwart of the Church. His bread was to be relied upon.

Careful Billy, a little old man with a flour-covered smock, a battered trilby and a patient old horse, was both a baker and a pig farmer. His horse and dray, from which he delivered bread, fowl corn, pig meal, etc., was a feature in the two villages.

The baker's cart and the farm cart

His horse jog-trotted, a sort of amble, and the four wheels of his dray rattled iron against stone on the cobbled road. Billy sat in front on a corn sack, the dray was covered by a tarpaulin sheet and open at the rear. In winter the wind must have whistled through from fore to aft but Careful Billy in his dusty flour-covered smock never wore an overcoat. He carried his name Careful Billy because, it was said, 'He had a good hiding as a boy for giving something away.' I found him extremely obliging. When he delivered fowl corn at our farmhouse he came with the bill already receipted.

Mother said, 'Now then, there is no need to pay. I have the receipt.' The little man, a serious little man, replied, 'Oh, Mrs Archer! Your name is worth more than that surely!'

Every sack, every piece of string Careful Billy owned was religiously taken care of. He delivered some fowl corn to a neighbouring farmer and was tipping the corn into a bin. He had trouble undoing the string off one of the sacks. The farmer took his penknife from his pocket saying, 'Let me cut the string.'

106

Careful Billy was quite upset. 'Look Sir,' he replied, 'I've had that piece of string for years, don't cut it. Give me time, I'll undo the knot.'

We used to have just one loaf off Billy on Saturdays, apart from fowl corn. Mother didn't like to give up that loaf although towards the end of Billy's baking career the loaves became a bit anaemic looking, a bit doughy.

Billy had a few large white sows and sold weaner pigs to cottagers. These 40 pound pigs would cost the cottager about £2 10s each. They always thrived after coming from this baker and dealer in pig meal. Then the villagers bought the rations for the

Smith's Stores, baker's and grocer's

cottage pig off Billy. He was a man for his time, who once made a special journey from Beckford to bring me 56 pounds of fowl corn.

Backing on to the Cotswolds and facing Bredon Hill is a cottage by the side of the main A485 Cheltenham Road known in my day as Pinch Loaf. I did know one lady who lived there who called it Hill View Cottage, but to me it will always be Pinch Loaf! At one time a baker used to live there too. He gave short weight in the 4 pound loaves of the day, and was prosecuted by the Weights and Measures people and so the cottage was given the name Pinch Loaf. This was many years ago, but the old folk of Ashton and Beckford knew where Pinch Loaf was. A German bomb fell across the road from the cottage in a field called Ram Acre. No one was injured but Pinch Loaf had a shaking.

CHAPTER FIFTEEN

HEDGES, DITCHES, POSTS AND RAILS

Mr Raymond Webb, a surveyor and land agent of Evesham, used to measure farm land for auctioneers and purchasers of land. Samuel Cope, the landlord of the old White Hart Inn at Ashton under Hill, was a reputed land measurer too, but how he acquired the skill I'm not sure. Measuring had to be exact and included everything. The term Hedges, Ditches, Posts and Rails was used by the surveyors who measured the farm land.

Measuring land to pay workmen who were on piece-work was not so exacting. Dad used a book published in the 1700s, a leather-bound little volume which I still have. This book of tables told the reader the size of a piece of land, for instance land ten chains long and one chain, or 22 yards, wide is an acre. Growing sprouts on the square, that is 3 feet one way and 3 feet the other, meant that it took 4,840 plants to the acre or 4,840 square yards. Allowing for wastage we pulled 5,000 sprout plants, which would plant an acre.

It is interesting to ponder and think of the folk who worked in local wood, the craftsmen who fashioned the gates, posts, hurdles and rails. Some years ago now the local paper published a comprehensive directory listing folk who lived in the villages. The Little Red Book was a mine of information. The surname was listed before the Christian name. I remember Moore, Charles, Ladder- and Hurdle-maker, Cotton, James, Water-diviner and Overthrow, Charles, Well-sinker. That amused me. I knew Mr Charles Overthrow. One or two were listed as Gentlemen.

Charles was a man who followed an old country craft, using materials all grown locally, everything, in fact, bar the nails. Hurdles are made with wood which is to hand – ash on the Cotswolds, withy in the vale, while in other areas the hazel wattle hurdle is common. Charles worked in withy, splitting the poles with a tool known as a cleaver which he hit with a wooden mallet known as a beetle, a Shakespearian name for a mallet. 'As thick as a beetle' is a saying used for someone three halfpence short of a shilling. The beetle with constant use becomes furred up at the edges, so anyone who scowls his eyebrows is 'beetle-browed'. The withy trees were pollarded, or cut, every seven years to provide poles suitable for hurdle-making. The trees then shoot more twigs which become poles. The saying is 'growth follows the knife' and it is amazing how a rough carpenter could fix wagon shafts or put a handle, or sned, on a scythe with wood grown and fashioned on the spot.

Green withy splits well for the rails and heads of hurdles. Red withy is useless for hurdles but makes the rungs of ladders. Charles had a stack of both varieties of withy alongside his thatched cottage and barn where the tools of his ancient trade were kept. A good hurdle-maker can make a dozen hurdles a day. Charles used cut nails like little chisels to secure the joints when the rails had been mortised into the uprights. Each nail was clenched.

There was always a great demand locally for Charles' ladders during the fruit-picking season. The ladders were made with sawn larch sides, using wood from the hill plantations, and red withy rungs or rounds, as they were called, from withy grown by the brook-side meadows. These ladders were strong and light-weight. The forty-rung job was used to pick the green walnuts (pickling walnuts) and the tall apple and pear trees. Charles also made a five-rung ladder for women to use blackberrying. Ladders for the rick-yard were strong and heavy. Some had oak rungs. Cottagers who kept pigs had pig ladders made by Charles to hang up their pig fresh from the pig bench when it was killed. A novelty I saw on a farm was a ladder made specially for haymaking. When the men unloaded the wagons they climbed up this ladder onto the load. The ladder was bow-shaped so that when the unloader wanted it out of his way he pushed it and it fell on the rick-yard floor. Being bow-shaped it came to no harm.

Another of Charles' products was what was known as a heaver. These were 10 feet long and took the place of a gate. They were made of larch and had five rails. The farmer drove in two worn horseshoes top and bottom of the gateposts. These acted like big staples and the top rail and bottom rail, which came out 'outspeeched by a foot', as we called it, were guided into these horseshoe staples. Heavers are useful when the gateway is only used occasionally.

So in these days of aluminium ladders and electric fences I like to think of Charles making his dozen hurdles a day and ladders to pick fruit from the tall apple trees which were once a feature of the orchards – no tidy rows of Cox's Orange Pippin half standards but tall trees of Normantons, Blenheims, and Warners King (known as Drunken Willy).

To me Charles Moore was more than the village hurdle-maker; he was an institution. At church Charles was parish clerk, sexton and verger. To listen to him doing the responses to the vicar gave a sense of meaning to the worship of our ancestors. He knew the Prayer Book like the back of his hand and the Amens always came at exactly the right moment.

As boys study their elders, and mock them at times, so we studied Charles Moore. It's how we learnt. At the end of the church service as the congregation filed from their pews to the darkness of a Sunday evening Charles, as he called it, 'doubted' the candle in the church with a great puff which sounded throughout the building. It was plain to everyone that the candles were being doubted. As sexton, this little man with a game leg buried the dead in the plot at the back of the church tower. As he grew older, Charles did have some help with the digging. I watched him in his yellow cords throwing up the clay from 6 feet down on those occasions. The day of the death of a villager Charles rang the Passing Bell which indicated the age of the man or woman who had passed over Jordan. This mournful exercise sent shivers down my spine when I was a child. As the vicar stood at the graveside reciting the funeral service, the coffin was lowered down on the webbing. When he came to those well-known words 'Ashes to ashes, dust to dust', it was then that Charles played an important part, sprinkling some soil on the coffin. Charles was not fussy in this ritual, the soil was not riddled and fine but plop, plop, plop – the clay resounded on the timber. We watched him fill in the grave when the mourners had left. Once he turned to a school friend of mine saying, 'How's your father?'

The man suffered from asthma badly, and the boy replied, 'Not very well, Mr Moore.'

'Tell him from me to hurry up and get better or else I'll have him in here.'

Charles was essentially a good man, although perhaps he lacked the sensitivity of others. On summer Sunday afternoons I've seen Charles sitting under his walnut tree reading his Bible – an old volume as big as a stable door.

One may rightly ask in what ways I most remember Charles. There are two: first, as a little man, said to be no more than 5 foot and a tater, walking lamely past our house on his way to the church and bell ringing; and secondly, in busy times, in Evesham working for a firm of ladder makers. He went to work on the same train that I took to school. His nickname was Stocky and we used to tease him. One summer evening Dad was mowing our lawn and Charles came by from the 7 o'clock train. Charles spotted me, standing by the front door, and said to Dad, 'That's the one who cheeked me this morning.'

Dad said just four words to me: 'Go in the house.'

Knowing what that meant I did as I was told. The broad leather belt was unfolded from Dad's waist and I felt the sting of leather against my backside. Of course I remember Charles Moore!

Wilf Grinnel mowing the field

Arthur Archer, his wife and son, lived in a remote Queen Anne grand stone house at the end of the wood, with stone mullion windows, a well of water and a garden. Besides being a gamekeeper, Arthur was a craftsman in wood. To see him swing the big felling axe, a tool so sharp, and chips like dinner plates coming away every few blows, was, to use a hackneyed phrase, poetry in motion.

He was a man and a half – 6 foot with a military bearing – and I spent hours in his company in the woods when I should have been working. The coops of broody pheasant hens with their young chicks in Staits Furlong are a pleasant memory. And I remember the day when Arthur shot a sparrow-hawk which had picked up one of his pheasant poults. The hawk fell dead, and the young pheasant was dead too, the talons of the hawk through its skull.

Arthur had served in the Artillery in the First World War and was subsequently deaf from the constant noise of the guns. He had

113

also farmed in Canada. His work in timber was quite special though. He made gates for the estate in the wood – little hunting gates, I remember. More than making gates, there is a skill in hanging a gate. Arthur told me how to make a gate fall to the post but said that to swing on a gate was to upset the fall. If you climb a gate which is locked, he said, always climb over at the instree not the head of a gate.

Arthur's gates were made of larch wood, an oak gate lasts longer but is much heavier. It is interesting that five-barred gates are just the height for a man to lean his elbows on and do what the poet W.H. Davies recommends: 'Stand and Stare'. John Masefield did just that. He wrote part of his well-known poem 'Everlasting Mercy' leaning on an oak gate which was hung during the Crimean War and lasted until 1930.

I've seen our shepherd leaning on a gate smoking his clay pipe and have smelt the Red Bell Shag tobacco as he watched his flock on the hill. A galloping shepherd is no use, he misses the fly-struck ewe, so the shepherd stood there watching his ewes and particularly the one where the maggots from the blowfly were causing it to twitch its tail, to run amok, to stand in the shade of the hedge.

The shepherd's dog, Rosie, drove the sheep into what is known as a slinget, a gore where the two hedges of the field came close together forming a triangle, a natural pen for the flock. He knew the struck ewe, caught it with his crook and dressed the wound made by the maggots.

There is a wooden gate at the side of a lane where I live. The gateway leads into a small field, the top of a coombe, where rabbits play in the morning sunshine. I used to smoke a pipe leaning on that gate, soaking up the atmosphere of the countryside. The other side of the lane is yellow with oil-seed rape in flower. There the gateway and the gate are so different. A metal contraption 15 feet wide stares coldly and graunches when it's swung on its hinges, setting your teeth on edge. The gate is wide to accommodate the combine harvester, factory made, a far cry from the gates made by Charles or Arthur.

CHAPTER SIXTEEN

THE TOP BRASS OF THE VILLAGES

My native village had been the home of the Baldwyn family for 500 years. The squires were lords of the manor until the end of the nineteenth century. It was then the village became lost for want of a leading family.

Around the vale Sir Francis Davies was at Elmley Castle, Sir Bolton Eyres Monsell at Dumbleton Hall. He later became Viscount Monsell and First Lord of the Admiralty. The Martins were at Overbury Court, and the big houses of Beckford were the homes of many important families. Hence the saying, if anyone in Ashton got a bit above themselves, 'Thee hast been to Beckford'.

It's true some folk retired to our village and had their names listed in the local directory as 'gentleman' but they were not natives like the Baldwyns. John Baldwyn lived with his wife, two bachelor sons and a daughter at The Croft, a little farm at the foot of Bredon Hill. His son Tom ran the farm and daughter Kate kept fowls and made butter. Over the centuries the family had come down in the world, having lived at one stage in splendour.

Bunch Baldwyn, a cousin who lived in St Barbara's Cottage, had her own unique presence. Full of good works she pottered along from cottage to cottage with jellies, blancmanges and beef tea. As an unpaid nurse and social worker she encouraged the old and infirm. Her special gift was remembering people in their hour of need.

Bunch was a kind eccentric, and how much poorer life would have been without her. Sometimes she gardened from daylight until

Elmley Castle Mill

dusk. Day after day the dirty crocks piled up in her kitchen until they were all used. Then followed a blitz of washing-up.

Working alongside Doctor Wellington, she acquired some skills in nursing and was a great believer in poulticing. One mustard plaster applied to Jack the rough carpenter's back did happen to be on the hot side. Oh yes, it cured Jack's lumbago but he lost some skin!

Bunch's cottage belonged to Archer and Bailey, Dad and his partner. Bunch came over to pay the rent on quarter days. She would arrive very late, a trait of the Baldwyns. We were allowed up as children to hear Bunch's stories of romance. It was fascinating – how the captain of the fire brigade, and the local policeman, courted her. It appeared that Bunch liked men in uniform!

This spinster of St Barbara's was afraid of thunder. If a storm seemed likely she would get my sister to stay with her overnight, and kept her spirits up drinking Woodpecker Cider.

I was bringing the cows in for milking one evening in summer with our cowman, Tom Whittle. It had been a lovely day. Seeing Bunch, Tom touched his cap and said, 'Good evening, Ma'am.'

She replied, 'Good evening, Mr Whittle. It's been a beautiful day.'

Tom, a great leg-puller, said, 'Yes, Ma'am. It's been a nice day.' He then looked up at the sky and added, 'I reckon we shall get some tempest tonight.'

He always called thunder tempest, and I reckon it spoiled Bunch's evening. She was round at our house soon after inviting my sister to stay the night with her.

Bunch was always proud of her ancestors and the number of Baldwyns that were in the vault by the church tower. She rests with them now and we must say 'God rest her soul'.

On the demise of the Baldwyn family another family became chief land owners and farmers in the village. Mr James Nicklin and family came from Smethwick in the Black Country.

The Nicklins were prosperous iron and steel manufacturers. It was a blessing in the village that the Nicklins took over where Squire Baldwyn left off. They were not country squires but they moulded into the village community very well indeed. The elder son, Bernard, had an inventive brain, producing a special steel at their factory for the First World War effort.

At The Close, at the foot of Bredon Hill, James Nicklin made a very special garden employing two gardeners. He had a liveried chauffeur who drove a Sunbeam car, something the locals had never seen before. Charles, the younger son, who had learnt farming under John Crump of Grafton, ran the farm.

The village benefited from the arrival of the Nicklin family. They worked well alongside the farming community in those First World War years. Nicklin's had shire-horses pulling their heavy iron and steel wagons on the streets of Birmingham and the Black Country. In time, these animals became tired of the street work, and they came to Ashton and had what to them was a holiday working on the farm. Some young horses broken in on the farm replaced them in Birmingham.

In those days, as a boy, James Nicklin seemed to me almost a king. He scared me in a way, although, as I found out in later life,

John Crump of Grafton. Bunch Baldwyn is standing by the gate

there was nothing scary about him. The fact was, as we schoolboys arrived at the station for the 8.50 train to town Tom Ellis, Nicklin's liveried chauffeur, drove the green Sunbeam car into the station yard. Mr Nicklin would emerge smoking a Churchill-sized cigar and buy a first-class ticket to Birmingham.

In the early 1920s James Curtis, who had been Food Minister for the Midlands, was knighted and became Sir James Curtis. He bought Elmwick House and Elmwick Cottage at Ashton, coming from Birmingham to our village. He and James Nicklin became great friends and together they made the village the envy of its neighbours.

James Nicklin bought an army hut soon after the First World War and gave it to the village, paying for it to be erected in his son's orchard. It was to be a village hall but never considered as common as that; it was called the Recreation Room. Hopkins of Dumbleton built it, and it's said that the men drank hogsheads of cider while putting it up. Ponto, who slept rough, carried the cider with a yoke and buckets from the Star Inn.

The two James's got their heads together, envisaging the village folk at dances, whist drives, socials and concerts.

'The young men need a club on winter evenings,' James Nicklin said.

Sir James replied, 'Ah, what they need is a billiard table. You have paid for the hall, and I shall buy the table for the young men.'

Sir James bought a full-sized billiard table, which was set up in a small room at the rear of the hall. It was a beauty, costing over £100 even in those days.

George Parminster, ex Royal Navy, was caretaker of the hall and he gave boxing lessons to the young men. A lady from Winchcombe taught dancing. The girls and fellows of the day attended her classes.

One market gardener forbad his daughter to go to the dancing class. He said, 'Where there's music and dancing there's the other job and there soon will be some bastard kids.' But the only girl who had what we call a Love Child was his daughter who never went dancing!

Nicklin provided a cricket field, one of the best in that day. Sir James Curtis, the President of the club, paid for a special pavilion; a room in the centre for teas; a room for the visiting team; another for the home team. All were painted white, and there was a yellow flag flying from the flag-pole.

The pavilion was opened on a sunny Saturday afternoon in the early 1920s. It was my lot as a small boy to present Sir James with a buttonhole while a bouquet of flowers was presented to Lady Curtis by a schoolfriend, Edna Cresswell. Oh, the scrubbing and grooming Mother put me through before the event! I provided the brilliantine, my favourite brand – Jockey Club. It was worth it, so it was said. As a footnote to the event, both Edna and I developed chicken-pox some days after. We had our legs pulled over that. What matter! I had given a buttonhole to a real Gentleman, a Sir who lived at Elmwick and who had the first WC in the village which emptied into what was known as a dumb well.

Sir James and Lady Curtis eventually disappeared. I don't know where – perhaps they returned to Birmingham. Mr Nicklin stayed until his death in his seventies but suffered as a result of the slump in the iron and steel industry, and the farming depression of the 1930s hit his agricultural business below the belt. He, like the Baldwyns, had to curb his life-style and his generosity to the village.

Mr Sidney Wesley Church, his wife and daughter came to live in Elmwick. Mr Church was a dentist with a practice in Evesham. He was a very well-spoken and well-dressed man, and he drove a car, something unusual in the 1920s. I remember one Wolseley he had with red leather upholstery. He even changed his car every year, which was unheard of.

What a thing to happen in those days, a real qualified dentist in the village. Previously, when suffering agonies with toothache, the only answer was the long, wooden-handled pliers, with no injection, in Doctor Roberson's surgery. Mr Church was a boon. I've known him extract teeth on his lawn on Sunday afternoons. Some folk were hard pressed to pay him, but he would say, 'Bring me a chip of your strawberries, or some of your peas.'

Mr Church threw himself into village activities. He was secretary of the War Memorial Committee, and involved in other such things. He was also a member of the Gentlemen's Club in Evesham. Oh, he was a handsome man, who could have been a film star. He died fairly young, a victim of asthma.

Mrs Church was schoolmistress at the village school for years. Village folk referred to her as The Governess. There were families in the 1920s who were poor, their children short of clothes and sometimes food. Mrs Church mothered these boys and girls. She organized rummage sales; she gave school Christmas parties, mainly at her own expense. There were no favourites at Mrs Church's school. In the summer-time, in fact most of the year when the weather was favourable, Mrs Church marched her pupils down the road to Church Close for rounders. A sporty type of lady, I can picture her today skipping up and down the Recreation Room to the dance tune 'Sir Roger de Coverley', played on the piano by one of the parents. Mrs Church was strict but kind. One boy I knew remembers how when he swore she washed his mouth out with soap and water. He spoke highly of her and of the Christmas presents she gave him.

The school was not academically brilliant, few pupils passed the scholarship exam, but they were happy leaving Mrs Church's school with a thorough grounding in the three Rs.

CHAPTER SEVENTEEN

SUNDAY –
SOMETHING SPECIAL

Of all the changes that have taken place in my lifetime none is more pronounced than the way we spend Sundays. The distractions of television, radio, videos and tape-recorders were quite unknown in the days when I was at school and Sunday in my home village of Ashton under Hill was always something special.

One way Sunday was special was how folks dressed. Afternoon walks along country lanes were permitted but only if the suit was a Sunday one and the shoes were polished. T-shirts and jeans, of course, were not obtainable in those days, but even if they had been we would never have worn them on a Sunday.

My Sunday started with all the family having breakfast together sitting up at the table. We would never stand in the kitchen with a cup of tea in one hand and a piece of toast in the other. We didn't have family prayers like some did. A friend of mine told me how at those morning exercises in devotion his father 'Gave God his orders for the day'.

On Sunday morning I would be wearing my black coat and waistcoat and my pinstripe trousers. My neck would be encased in an Eton Collar, tight and cutting. Wearing an overall to keep me clean I shelled the peas, and scraped the potatoes for Sunday lunch, dinner we called it.

At 10.15 we were off to Sunday school in the village chapel. Every child in our village went to Sunday school and it was good compared with day school. We sang Sankey hymns with gusto,

A Sunday school outing on the Malvern Hills

accompanied by a harmonium and a viola. When our names were called on the register we answered 'Present'. Mr Cotton, our superintendent, would be listening and if some boy or girl failed to answer he would often know the reason for their absence and perhaps say, 'Ah, her mother's not well and she will be looking after her.' He would nod to his son, whose job it was to call the register, saying, 'Put domestic after her name. Give her her mark.'

After dinner I usually went for a walk on Bredon Hill with my friend, Geoff. Sometimes we would climb the hill as far as the Summer-house, or Parsons Folly, and tease the Wild Man of the Hill, Joe Green, trying to get him to let us climb the tower of the Summer-house without paying him the two pence he charged. He chased us down the hill. Luckily Geoff and I were pretty fleet of foot after Saturdays with Charlie Heath the football trainer, who organized paper chases or hare and hounds on the hill.

Sunday tea was special, with bottled pears from a Kilner Jar, or a tin of Roman Gold Apricots and some of Grandma's cake.

The hermit of Bredon Hill

The chapel service was at 6 o'clock. The old chapel had been Baptist but the new one, built in 1924, was a Free Church. The preachers were varied. It could be a Quaker, a Methodist, a Baptist, a member of the Brethren – one never knew. Perhaps we should not have gone to church for entertainment, but Sundays were dull. I did have one or two favourite preachers, however.

Reuben Marshall, a fruit and vegetable merchant, came from Pershore, either on a bicycle or some primitive motor bike or trike, a three-wheeled affair with a carrier on the front to transport his fruit and vegetables. He was a dark, swarthy man with a Ghandi haircut and a heart of gold. His favourite subject was 'Shadrach, Meshach and Abednego in the burning fiery furnace'. Half-way through his sermon he would remember to take off his cycle clips, then in summer-time he would ping his braces, which made snapping noises as the webbing hit his chest. His prayer was a gem: 'We worship thee tonight, Lord, not only in Cathedrals, Temples and Tabernacles but in Churches, Chapels and Bethels up and down our land and under the canopy of the Glorious Heavens.' A generous man, Reuben gave without stint to every good cause and to the poor. He sheltered a widow woman in his house saving her from the workhouse.

Fred Bubb was a Quaker, a jolly man with a smile. He had a market garden near Evesham. He cycled over on those Sunday nights in summer, and I can picture him now as he parked his bike in the coal-house and entered the vestry mopping his brow. Fred shared his time with the hierarchy of the Society of Friends, the Cadburys in particular. He did seem to have an ear and an eye for depth of character. One Sunday he recalled a Quaker meeting where a very eloquent doctor was the speaker.

'What did you think of the doctor this morning?' he was asked as he left the meeting.

'Well,' Fred replied, 'The doctor was very good but I had the blessing from what that old ploughman said.'

Fred spent a season harvesting in Canada. He went there on doctor's orders for health reasons, leaving his market garden in the

Emmanuel Jones, local preacher

hands of his wife. He told the story more as a talk than as one of his sermons. He was returning from Canada on one of the ocean liners. It was Sunday morning. The piano was playing and the folk were singing music-hall songs. This didn't seem right to Fred Bubb, a man who used to say his name was all Bs but U. He asked the captain if they could have something more appropriate as it was Sunday. The captain agreed that there could be some hymn singing and Fred gave out the hymn-books. Fred had his cornet with him and said he would accompany the singing. He asked if anyone had a favourite hymn and one man suggested a number in the hymn-book which was 'Now the day is over'. It was ten o'clock in the morning but Fred said, 'I've never heard it sung any better.'

William Boulton, manager of a multiple store in town, came in his Wolseley car. Handsome, nicely dressed in grey tweed, he jingled his silver in his trouser pocket as he gave the address. He was an eloquent preacher, a man who treated the Gospel as it is meant, as Good News. His favourite topic was taken from some words spoken, I gather, by St Paul: 'Our light affliction which is but for a moment is nothing to be compared with the Glory which is to come.'

Edward Davies, a blacksmith, was a Welshman. When he got carried away in his sermon he spoke in what is known as the Hywl, a singsong voice peculiar to the Welsh. Edward was a bit doleful when he said Jonah was in the whale's belly three days and three nights. One Sunday he said Jeremiah was called the doleful prophet because he wrote the Book of Lamentations.

I liked the truly local preachers – the men of the land and the forge. They rang true and gave of their great experience. I didn't care much for the so-called missioners. One of these, black-suited and solemn, came to convert the village. He raised his voice, cried and danced around the rostrum. One evening he caught his foot against the collection basket and kicked it up the aisle past me. 'Filthy lucre!' he cried – and I wasn't supposed to laugh!

The shouting and crying was part of the act of some, but I did object to the way these men, and we knew little of their background, would buttonhole folk as they went through the door at the end of the service. 'Are you saved?' they would ask. That was really a private thing between man and God.

One of the treats of chapel in the 1920s was when Revd Harry Soan came over to preach from Atch Lench Baptist church, near Evesham. Harry, a handsome lean man, a thinker, a philosopher and one of nature's gentlemen, had been a minister at a group of Cotswold Baptist churches. At Atch Lench Harry's flock were mostly smallholders, growing their strawberries, asparagus, onions and plums. Their wives worked on the land, picking and tying for their husbands. They were all paid a wage by their husbands for their work. Harry told me that in a season of bad prices at the market the smallholders would be in debt to their wives, who had to wait until the following year for part of their wages. I had never heard of this system before. Maybe it was peculiar to that area.

That well-known family the Bomfords supported the village chapels as they had done for hundreds of years, way back to the days of the Commonwealth. There were in fact so many Bomfords at one time that when the famous preacher Revd C.H. Spurgeon visited the villages he sat down to a meal with no fewer than seventy Bomfords. He remarked afterwards that Worcestershire should be called Bomfordshire.

Revd Soan's visits to our village chapel were memorable. He had a sense of humour and could tell a joke in the pulpit, an unusual attribute to many of the sober-sides who came. This had an influence on a boy in his teens and I saw that Harry Soan's Gospel was quite attractive.

Every July in Ashton a strawberry and cream tea was held at Old Manor Farmhouse by Dad's partner, Mr Harry Bailey and Mrs Bailey. The event was to raise money for a new village chapel. The tables were arranged on Mr Bailey's croquet lawn and the strawberries grown by Dad and Mr Bailey. The cream came from our dairy of Shorthorn cows. The helpings of both fruit and cream were enormous. Stalls laden with home-made articles encircled the lawn, and Harry Soan came over with a party of Baptists from Atch Lench and Harvington. I remember seeing Revd Soan sitting under Mr Bailey's Wellingtonia tree with other men in dog collars discussing religion, and I'd guess politics if Harry had his way. He was smoking a large pipe, the eddies of smoke rising like a garden couchgrass fire among the fundamentalist religious ministers of the Vale of Evesham. Smoking, like drinking, was taboo but Harry was radical and remained so.

After tea, when the stalls were cleared and the produce sold, came the speeches or addresses by the ordained ministers who had come from churches in the vale. Suitable topics on these occasions were those of a spiritual nature rather than worldly. When Harry Soan took the stage on the steps of Mrs Bailey's dovecote he had his own ideas. This young man who ministered among the little mastermen of the land told us a story I still remember. He spoke of boys starting work in factories, on the land and at the big houses of the vale.

'A boy,' he said, 'had just started in service at a big house serving under the footman and the butler. A lord came to stay and it was the duty of the boy to take shaving water to the important visitor's bedroom. He was very nervous and practised the words he had to say when he went up to the room. He was told that when he knocked on the door of the bedroom the gentleman would say "Who is it?" The boy was to reply, "It's the boy, my Lord, with the shaving water." The lad was so nervous that when he eventually knocked on the door and heard a sharp, loud voice say "Who is it?" he replied "It's the Lord, my boy, with the shaving water."'

Harry Soan left the ministry some years ago now and took a farm high up on the Black Mountains in Wales. He kept speckle-faced Welsh sheep on 108 acres. 'In the spring a young man's fancy lightly turns to thoughts of love,' he would say. 'My rams have different ideas, they only think of love in the autumn as the days grow shorter.'

When I last saw him ten years ago he had retired and was what I call a seasoned man in his eighties, a talented broadcaster on country matters and a storyteller. He and his wife lived a simple life away from the supermarkets and all the noise of modern evolution. He joined the Iona Community and seemed happy in some ways, yet very conscious of the tide of events in our nuclear age.

At his mountain home Harry looked back on his time in the Vale of Evesham, recalling the people who were in his flock before he left the ministry. Listening to Harry and his wife recalling life as it was sixty years ago brought to mind words of the Silver King: 'Oh God, put back the universe and give me yesterday.'

CHAPTER EIGHTEEN

THE REVERS OF ELMLEY

Frederick Revers and family came to Elmley Castle in 1912. They made their home at The Mill, an inn on the outskirts of the beautiful village. In those days the inn was a cider house, the cider being made on the premises.

Fred Revers was a Cotswold man coming from farming stock near Broadway. Before he came to Elmley he was head keeper for the Earl of Anglesey on Cannock Chase. He was a great sportsman who loved his gun and his dogs. He organized many spaniel trials. Barbara, his wife, provided the lunches for the guns and the beaters when they lived in Staffordshire. They had eight children, four boys and four girls. Two daughters survive, Mary and Marjorie. Mary has been playing the organ in Great Comberton church for seventy-four years.

I knew the youngest son, Cyril, very well. He was an idol of mine on the cricket field, one of the best batsmen in our village team. In the 1920s some village cricket players turned out in grey flannels, with pancake caps and so on. Cyril always looked the part in his nicely creased cream flannels and shirt, and the blue and gold members' cap. This fine looking young man also played hockey for Worcestershire. He had a particularly fine voice and sang in the church choir too. All this does suggest that Cyril was a gentleman farmer. Although it's true he was a gentleman and a farmer, in the 1920s such men had to roll their sleeves up and work with the men. Cyril won a scholarship to Prince Henry's Grammar School at Evesham, the first pupil from Elmley school to gain a place.

Cyril Revers

In that day and age, when horses and ponies were as commonplace as cars are today, Cyril had a pony and rode it the five miles to school, stabling it at the Northwick Hotel at the other end of the town. I can picture this lad cantering along the wide grass verge at Hinton on the Green on his way to school, bumping in the saddle, his satchel bouncing on his back. When I went to that school Cyril had left, but Marjorie, the youngest daughter, was still attending. She used to keep goal for the hockey team. Cyril was often on Hinton station platform when I came home on the 4 o'clock train. He would come and talk to us as the train stood in the station. His name being Revers, we would cheek him and sing, 'Way down upon the Swanney Rever'.

At that time Fred Revers was umpire for Ashton cricket team. An imposing figure, he would sit on a shooting-stick as the overs were bowled. He was dressed in tweeds, brown tweeds and tweed plus-fours. Dad was friendly with him but as a boy he seemed awe-inspiring to me. Working for gentry like the Earl of Anglesey had given him a presence.

Fred Revers was a tenant to General Sir Francis Davis and farmed The Hall Farm at Bricklehampton. General Davis came from a long line of military men, stretching right back to Corunna. Like his father before him, he lived at Elmley and had an estate there. He had great loyalty to Church and State and a keen sense of humour. During the First World War the local MP was Lieutenant Commander Eyres Monsell. General Davis sent a message to him when he, Eyres Monsell, was serving in the Mediterranean. It read as follows: 'If you don't strafe the enemy any more than you have recently I shan't vote for you at the next election.'

All the tenants on the general's estate were given a brace of pheasants when the shoots were held on the land which stretched

A shoot with Fred Revers

Fred Revers perched on his shooting-stick

from way up Bredon Hill to Great Comberton. When Lady Davis took the birds to Fred Revers she remarked with a little smile, 'I suppose this is like bringing coals to Newcastle.' The Revers family lived on the land with their guns and I gather they were never short of game for the pot.

Fred Revers farmed Tibbets Farm, Little Comberton, with his two sons, Cyril and Walter. Walter was a very talented stockman; he bred Hereford bulls for the pedigree sales and also ran a herd of Red Poll cattle. It seems that Walter, unlike Cyril, had never the time for sport. It's like that with the seven-days-a-week men, who live and work with animals. Cyril, the younger brother, was in charge of the arable side. He grew the corn, built the ricks, employed a lot of labour, market gardening with sprouts and beans and peas which were harvested piece-work.

On the other side of the hill from the Revers' farm, at Bricklehampton, was the scene that inspired Sir Arthur Quiller-Couch to write the following poem:

ODE

UPON ECKINGTON BRIDGE,
RIVER AVON

O Pastoral heart of England! like a psalm
    Of green days telling with a quiet beat —
O wave into the sunset flowing calm!
    O tired lark descending on the wheat!
Lies it all peace beyond that western fold
    Where now the lingering shepherd sees his star
Rise upon Malvern? Paints an Age of Gold
    Yon cloud with prophecies of linked ease —
Lulling this land, with hills drawn up like knees,
    To drowse beside her implements of war?

Man shall outlast his battles. They have swept
    Avon from Naseby Field to Severn Ham;
And Evesham's dedicated stones have stepped
    Down to the dust with Montfort's oriflamme.
Nor the red tear nor the reflected tower
    Abides; but yet these eloquent grooves remain
Worn in the sandstone parapet hour by hour
    By labouring bargemen where they shifted ropes.
E'en so shall man turn back from violent hopes
    To Adam's cheer, and toil with spade again.

Ay, and his mother Nature, to whose lap
    Like a repentant child at length he hies,
Not in the whirlwind or the thunder-clap
    Proclaims her more tremendous mysteries:
But when in winter's grave, bereft of light,
    With still, small voice divinelier whispering

134

– Lifting the green head of the aconite,
   Feeding with sap of hope the hazel-shoot –
She feels God's finger active at the root,
   Turns in her sleep, and murmurs of the Spring.

The Revers' land, on the north side of Bredon Hill, is clay and difficult to farm. It took four horses in line to plough it. Bill Reed worked on the farm as carter for sixty-five years and was presented with a long-service medal at the Three Counties Show. Bill would leave the stable at 7 o'clock on winter mornings with a plough-boy to drive the four-horse team, the foremost, the lash horse, the body horse and the filler. They would plough all day that yellow clay which turned over like liver, but when the frost laxed it would grow heavy crops of wheat and beans. The lighter land grew the sprouts and the peas. A ploughman's lunch, or bait, under the hedge bottom at 10 o'clock provided a welcome break. Then they would work through until 3 o'clock and then go home to dinner. This avoided the problem of shutting off the teams at 1 o'clock and then working in the afternoon. Fred Revers kept several teams of fine shire-horses because, ploughing that sort of land, you could work for a full day yet cover less than an acre.

I knew Bill Reed, he was interested in my earlier books. In the Queen Elizabeth pub one evening he said to me, 'I want to have a word with you about a chap you wrote about in your book. You said what a fine man George so and so was. Well, he was that crooked he couldn't lie straight in bed.'

I laughed replying, 'George so and so was a pseudonym, a made-up name. If you knew someone of that name, it is quite incidental.'

Bill Reed left the rural scene some years ago but A.E. Housman gives a good word picture of Bill in his poem 'Is my Team Ploughing?'.

Bill Reed, the Revers' carter

136

IS MY TEAM PLOUGHING?

Is my team ploughing,
That I was used to drive
And hear the harness jingle
When I was man alive?

Ay, the horses trample,
The harness jingles now;
No change though you lie under
The land you used to plough.

Is football playing
Along the river shore,
With lads to chase the leather,
Now I stand up no more?

Ay, The ball is flying,
The lads play heart and soul;
The goal stands up, the keeper
Stands up to keep the goal.

The day of the four-horse team is gone for ever. No more carters hang their frail baskets on the hames of the foremost horse on the way to the ploughing or with shut links mend the broken traces. These men considered their animals, slipping stockings full of sheep's wool under their collars to ease a sore shoulder. They stole linseed cake from the shepherd's store to feed the horses, making their coats shine.

Back at Hall Farm Marjorie Revers worked on the land while Mary Revers taught at the local school. With pony and trap Marjorie would take food and drink to the harvesters. Later she also began rearing turkeys. A giant incubator taking two thousand eggs hatched out the broad-breasted white turkeys for sale around

Marjorie Revers and her niece

Worcestershire as poults. At Christmas the local women were busy plucking and dressing birds for the seasonal market.

The breeding of Hereford cattle predominated over everything else at Chapel Farm, Netherton, an offshoot of Elmley, where Mr Stevens farmed. He was a contemporary of Fred Revers, and Mary Revers was friendly with his housekeeper. The Stevens were a great asset to the village of Elmley, providing playing fields for the village children. The one son kept falcons. I remember one escaped on to our land at Kersoe and young Mr Stevens captured it. Mr Compton, the man in charge of the pedigree herd of Hereford cattle, was kingpin in the Stevens' enterprise. He judged cattle at the shows and sales in Britain and abroad. Having seen many pedigree Hereford stock in shows and sales about Bredon I can say that I have never seen animals to surpass those bred by Mr Stevens. To say they were dark red in colour is an understatement. Stevens' Herefords were the colour of oxblood and stood low on the ground. Animals with such conformity are always in great demand. A bull bred by Mr Stevens by the name of Ringer fetched £9,000 early in the century.

Dad and his partner bought a Stevens' bull to serve our Shorthorn cows about 1930. The bull sold at Gloucester market for 40 guineas, a fair price in those days. We led it to the station and put it in a cattle truck to travel the 20 miles to Beckford station. It was a dark winter's night when I walked with our cowman, Tom Whittle, to collect the bull at Beckford and take it along the 2 miles home. Lantern in hand we walked with the young Hereford up Rabbit Lane to Ashton. I was surprised how easily the animal travelled on the halter, but of course Stevens' cattle would have been exercised and led on the halter.

Fred Revers

We had not had the bull at the farm many weeks before we had a visit from some Russians who wanted to buy it from us. It appeared that the agriculturalists from the Russian Government had purchased some stock from Mr Stevens and were still short of another bull. I don't know what profit was offered to my father by these folk but we kept the bull, which proved to be an excellent stock-getter.

Back in the 1920s something that was always rammed home by the farmers of the day was that farming cannot be learnt from a book. Agricultural colleges were frowned upon by some. Mr Stevens was a progressive man. His buildings were superb, animals well housed and he was a pioneer in the making of silage. He made the silage in towers, the green herbage pitched into the towers by hand. Labour intensive, yes, but then labour was cheap. A demonstration was organized at Chapel Farm to show the farmers of the Evesham Vale how to make silage. Dad and his partner went that day. Both were always interested in new ideas and this certainly was new to them. I remember that tea-time when I had returned home from school, Dad explained to me what he had seen that day. Yes, the grass was green as it went into the silos and compressed down, getting quite hot. He saw cattle being fed by the silage made earlier in the year and they were enjoying it. But, oh, it smelled sour, he said. I remember his words and how wrong he was. He said, 'It will never catch on.'

Like keeping hens in deep litter, silage-making was in its infancy in those days and the old saying 'Good hay hath no fellow' was the rule.

CHAPTER NINETEEN

LADY NORAH AND
THE POOR LAW

The year was 1928, my third year at Prince Henry's Grammar
School at Evesham. Ashton under Hill, my native village, was then
in Gloucestershire but villagers who were unlucky enough to be
taken to the workhouse went to Hampton Workhouse near
Evesham in Worcestershire. This is now the site of Avonside
Hospital, known then as Hampton Adlum, or Headland.

The large gardens had rich soil known as the Abbey Land, part
of the Abbey complex, black and fertile. Here the inmates grew the
vegetables for the house and the surplus was fed to the pigs – very
good economy. Dad was a member of the Guardians Committee.
They had a representative in every parish to advise the Relieving
Officer, who dealt with relief to the poor, and the workhouse
master, who was in charge of the inmates.

Two men from Ashton under Hill were in Evesham workhouse
and had been for years. One I remember was known as Spider
Winnet. These men between them worked in the gardens and Spider
looked after the pigs. Other men from Gloucestershire were in the
Evesham house, including two from Aston Somerville where Lady
Norah Fitzherbert was the Guardian. Without any notice or warning
the powers-that-be whisked these four men away to Cheltenham
workhouse so that the Gloucestershire ratepayers would keep them.
Lady Norah came over to our house in her car, explained the
problem and said how unhappy the men were in the big workhouse
in Cheltenham, with no gardening and no pig-keeping.

Dad drove to Cheltenham and saw the men who begged him to get them back to Evesham. Looking back at parish records it is odd that the authorities ignored something which happened in the 1830s. It is said in our Vestry Book that two cottages at Ashton under Hill were sold to provide money to help to build the workhouse infirmary at Evesham.

The workhouse master at Cheltenham said that he could release the men as vagrants and if Dad took them to Evesham the workhouse master there would be obliged to accept them in the casual ward.

Next morning the Cheltenham workhouse master released the men at 9.30. They knew the road to Evesham and walked as far as the Cheltenham racecourse where Dad picked them up in his car. It was during the Christmas holidays from school and the four men had cocoa and bread and cheese in our farmhouse kitchen on their way to Evesham workhouse. They were just like school boys coming home. Their weathered faces shone. Cheltenham had been so impersonal compared with their stay in Evesham, where they felt a part of the system.

At the next meeting of the Guardians, Dad and Lady Norah had their way; the men should stay at Evesham. On 31 March 1931, Ashton under Hill and Ashton Somerville became part of Worcestershire, the boundary being altered.

The old Poor Law system had many faults. One was that a man and his wife were not allowed to live together in the workhouse. This made a mockery of the marriage service which states, 'Those whom God hath joined together let no man put asunder.'

Although the Guardians would pay rates there were so few ratepayers in the villages in the old days. This made the parish relief pay mean. One autocratic Guardian used to say to the poor, 'I'll pay you half a crown a week.' If they said it was not enough he would reply, 'There is always the House [the workhouse]'.

Memories of the workhouse make me feel sure that the Guardians of the Poor who lived in the village knew as a rule which of the villagers were needy. Every Christmas Dad and his partner, Mr Harry Bailey, caught enough rabbits on Bredon Hill for the workhouse inmates to have a rabbit pie supper.

I went to a party at the workhouse; it was known as the Rabbit Pie Supper and Entertainment. Here was sex discrimination, as it's known today. Men and women sat separately on either side of the hall for the entertainment. A play, 'The Burgomaster's Daughter', was performed by a group from Evesham. It was received with applause by the inmates. The dress of the men that evening was tidy, grey fustian suits; the women wore plain grey dresses. The workhouse master gave presents of pipes and tobacco for the men, and the women had presents of some sort also.

As a boy of thirteen I well remember that evening at the workhouse. After the performance, a party of dancers entertained the inmates. One lady in particular, who performed under the pseudonym of Vera, made the old men clap and laugh. Vera had style, and her acts were both clever and funny. Among the guests that evening were, of course, the Guardians and among them were two notable characters, a maiden lady and an ex-mayor of the town. They sat together not far from where Dad and I were sitting. When Vera showed rather a lot of leg and cleavage the two Guardians shaded their eyes with the programme. This tickled me pink and Dad smiled.

No change of name could have made the workhouse acceptable to the poor. It was called The Poor House, House of Maintenance, House of Protection or a Bettering House; later it became The Public Assistance Institution.

I do wonder, now the casual wards are closed, where the vagrant traveller goes for shelter. The casual ward was not ideal yet it gave a roof to men, or shall I say the 'gentlemen of the road'. I used to meet a lot of these men as they rested on their way to Tewkesbury or Cheltenham. They used to brew up billycans of tea in a shed near the turnpike at Ashton. These men were often ex-soldiers of the First World War, ragged but still showing their medals. When they walked the main road they walked one on either side, looking for cigarette ends thrown from cars to put in their clay pipes. Some smoked tea leaves. These tramps picked the peas every summer, went into city lodging houses in winter and sold matches at street corners. When I hear of all the strikes today I still think of the parish poor of sixty-five years ago.

It was folk like Lady Norah Fitzherbert who made life more bearable for the poor in the 1920s. She and her husband, William, farmed the land on their estate at Aston Somerville. Alexander Dyke was their farm manager. When he came there from farming under Bredon Hill he brought with him his knowledge as a professional breeder of Shorthorn cattle. The Fitzherbert Shorthorn herd was well known on the Cotswolds and in the Vale of Evesham.

The Fitzherberts, being bona fide farmers, didn't dabble in market gardening but every year they grew a field of brussel sprouts which were auctioned in August and bought by the Evesham merchants.

Lady Norah was an expert gardener, and the gardens at Aston Somerville were a picture all year round. How she got the idea one doesn't know, but to protect her valuable, delicate plants she had straw brought in from the farm which she used to thatch over some of them. As a supporter of the Nursing Association Lady Norah held meetings and tea-parties at her house and gardens.

In all she was an example of generosity and caring for the poor of the parish, which she did in her quiet way. It was like social security but done privately, by someone who was a real lady.

CHAPTER TWENTY

THE SEXTYS OF BANGROVE

Tucked under the Cotswold Edge at Bangrove lived a family which was a legend earlier this century. In fact the Sexty's roots went back much further.

The two remaining members of the family as I knew them were William, approaching his 100th year, and Lucy, who was eighty-six. William was a short and stocky character, a typical yeoman farmer, breeched and gaitered, dressed in good Cotswold tweed and a black and white check waistcoat. His chin, covered with a bristly beard, jutted forward from the Cromwellian round head. There was something of the rural aristocrat about him. To see him sitting in the ingle-nook of his stone farmhouse and listen to the music of his true Gloucestershire brogue was an inspiration. He was a man who knew his land intimately and was a very good stock-breeder, particularly of his shire-horses. His favourite was a black stallion which he named Carburettor, related to another famous animal called Harold. William travelled this stallion, Carburettor, around the north Cotswolds and the Vale of Evesham. The stallions were shown off to the local farmers at cattle markets in April before their perambulations serving the mares. I remember watching William Sexty with Carburettor at Beckford market and thinking what a fine animal he was.

It is interesting to note a brief history of the development of the shire-horse. Way back at the time of the Norman Conquest the horses, used by the Normans, were improved by some imported from Flanders, and when plate armour reached its greatest weight in the time of Henry VIII the animals had to carry four hundredweight. In the eighteenth century Arthur Young mentions the Old English Black Horse or the Black Horse of the Midlands, and more imports from the Low Countries resulted in the majestic animal of today, big framed, deep chested with strong legs and hair or feathers on its fetlocks, silky rather than woolly. In 1878 the English Cart-horse Society was founded. This became known as the Shire-horse Society in 1884. As a young man William Sexty was one of the first breeders of the genuine shire-horse.

This, however, is the history of Carburettor and Harold. Their offspring worked on the farms until they were five or six years old, when the farmers were tempted to sell them to the brewers and railway companies for town work pulling heavy drays.

It was on a May morning when I was cycling back from Beckford, having at ten years of age just learnt to ride a bike, when I met William Sexty with Carburettor. The stallion had been to serve mares in our village. I didn't know then, and maybe lots of folk may not know today, that it is proper to lead a horse on the right-hand side of the road, the idea being that if the horse was frightened by traffic it would jump towards the hedge. William approached me with his horse on the right-hand side of the road. There was just room for me to cycle between the horse and the grass verge, and as I did I said, 'You are on the wrong side of the road.'

Mr Sexty swiped at me with his stick and called me a cheeky mortal. Dad explained to me afterwards that he was in the right.

Next year at Beckford market Mr Sexty was there with his entire, as the farm men called a stallion. Its sleek black coat shone, its great hooves clip-clopped over the rough limestone road outside the inn. The brass on its mullion, or bridle, shone like gold, perfection in horse flesh bred by William's careful selection. That year Carburettor came and served Flower, our liver chestnut mare. The colt, Turpin, was perhaps the biggest gelding on the farm where I grew up.

William Sexty was a devout Methodist who entertained the preachers for Sunday lunch and tea when they visited the little chapel. A friend of mine, a local preacher, used to have tea with him and Lucy. He said it was like going back in time to visit this man, who was then in his late eighties. The Shorthorn herd that had been on the farm since his youth was down to a few cows by then.

My friend watched William on summer Sundays after chapel drive a flock of turkeys from his stubble field to the turkey house. William and Lucy would top the market with their birds at Christmas, the Mammoth Bronze turkeys of yesterday.

One day unfortunately, William's kind of farming would have to end. He had ridden with the hounds, kept the pantry supplied with the partridges off the stubble, and made hogsheads of cider and perry the old-fashioned way – a little pony turning the stone on a trough of cider apples, the juice pressed and the pommace used to bank up the labourers' fires in winter.

But William's time was not yet over. Although in his nineties he still had spirit. Lucy, at eighty-six, had the grace of a debutante. Her mind went back to years ago and she recalled her sister and two girls from neighbouring farms and herself as they danced for joy under the trees in the meadows. We sang to the dance, she said simply, evocatively, it was all the music we wanted.

This attractive girl never married but decided to stay and look after her bachelor brothers. She talked of farmhouse housewifery, city airs and graces, as she showed off her cream lace dress. Then back to farming. Mares being taken to the stallion, a hundred turkeys being driven down the lane into the stubble and Miss Lucy following with a red flag.

William and Lucy continued a low-key type of farming until the approach of William's one hundredth birthday. The tree-shadowed stone farmhouse in the woods had been a hive of industry, and inside it hadn't changed. The pot hook still swung the big kettle over the fire to heat the water for tea. In the spring the scent of the lilac came through the mullioned window as the logs burnt on a bed of ashes and William told his story in his musical dialect. But winter evenings around the fire were when William was at his best.

William had a tradition of celebrating his birthday in mid-summer, and when his one hundredth birthday came round, and he received a telegram from the king, he held a party in the garden. The farm had now ceased to function. Under the lime trees the implements of old-time farming rusted among the nettles, the cattle stalls were empty, the turkeys had gone, and there were only photographs of Carburettor to remind William of his famous stallion, but his birthday was celebrated in style. Neighbours had mown the lawn, the flowers were all in their summer splendour, the trestle tables were loaded with the best farmhouse fare. His sister, only two years his junior, had baked a birthday cake.

William, in check suit and linen waistcoat, spoke for a while replying to a toast given by Bernard Miles, a very old friend of the family. William spoke of harvests of yields of hay and corn, of wet summers, of marriage, which he told the party he had never bought a ticket for. The party that year was on a Sunday, and William was very particular on Sunday observance. Bernard Miles said, 'I'm going to take your photo, William.'

William replied, 'Not on a Sunday, you won't.'

The photo taken by Bernard that Sunday shows William with his hand across his face. I've seen that picture, showing the religious conviction of a man of principles.

'Shall I read to you?' Bernard Miles asked William.

'Yes,' he replied.

'What shall I read?'

'Just read from the book over there. Read Corinthians, chapter 13.'

Bernard read the passage which William had selected:

Though I speak with the tongues of men and of angels, and have not charity, I am become as sounding brass, or a tinkling cymbal. When I was a child, I spake as a child, I understood as a child, I thought as a child, but when I became a man, I put away childish things. For now we see through a glass darkly but then face to face: Now I know in part; but then I shall know even as I am known. And now abideth faith, hope, and charity, these three; but the greatest of these is charity.

This could be called William's testimony on his hundredth birthday. It was his last party; the following winter he died. The house remains, the walnut tree, the perry pear trees. William is remembered, for with his departure went a bit of the history of the farm on that rare bit of country which lies between the Cotswolds and the Vale of Tewkesbury.

CHAPTER TWENTY-ONE

LEN SPIRES AND THE FAMILY FARM

The Spires family were neighbours of ours and have lived in Ashton under Hill for centuries. They were even mentioned as small farmers in the Enclosures Act of 1783.

Apart from farming the family also did a lot of haulage work with their horses when the village roads were surfaced by the MacAdam process introduced by the Scot, MacAdam, late in the eighteenth century. What a sight it was to see Spires' strawberry roan cart-horse in the shafts of the water cart, and the heavy, puffing steamroller with a brass lion on the front of the boiler going backwards and forwards repairing the country lanes. Road-making without tar and granite chippings simply meant laying large local limestones on the bottom, with smaller ones rolled in by a steamroller. Over this a mixture of sand, gravel, crushed limestone, and water was rolled in to make a cement-free concrete. It's true that those lanes were often muddy in winter and dusty in summer but the making and repairing of them was good to watch if you had time to stand and stare. The stone all came from Bredon Hill, broken by Joe Barnett.

The Spires were a versatile family of little master men – farmers, market gardeners, hauliers and even bricklayers. Len's father, William Richard, was a great friend of my father and they attended the village school together. I can still remember Dad, black suited, returning from his friend's funeral. At sixteen Len was a strong young man, easily able to handle the two and a quarter hundredweight sacks of corn. He was a young yeoman of the best

Len Spires at work on the farm

sort, with a very subtle sense of humour. After his father's death he worked the small farm himself and grew market garden crops which were harvested by the family. He usually grew a few late sprouts ready for market in the hungry month of March. He kept a few pigs and a house cow, the latter being brought yearly to our Hereford bull for service.

The family picked the strawberries and I remember Len's mother bringing a couple of pounds of magnificent Royal Sovereigns to us as neighbours. The fruit was wrapped in a rhubarb leaf which I thought was a good temporary container. Len, who was some years older than me, was quite a reasonable footballer, but not in the same class as his brother Martin, who was captain of the local team. Another old friend of mine, who used to play football in the village team, once made this comment about Len, 'When we played an away game and had an after match drink in Cheltenham we were never afraid of anyone if Len was with us.' A quiet, gentle man who could hold his own with anybody, Len had two important attributes, strength of character and physical strength.

Folk like Len never made newspaper headlines or served on the parish council, but he worked quietly on, drilling, planting, horse hoeing, hand hoeing and gathering his crops. A barrel of cider stood in the cart shed, hens ran free range around the buildings and on the muck bury, and the produce of the market garden was stacked at the roadside ready for collection by the market lorry.

A day at Beckford market with friends as a few of the cattle reared by the Spires' family were sold, or maybe a visit to an agricultural show or a football match were the extent of Len's holidays. There was no 40 hour week at Glebe Farm where the Spires had scratched the top 6 inches of soil for generations. It was a way of life which went on year after year almost unaltered.

Things changed for Len when arthritis disabled his leg but he still plodded on. No doubt the back-breaking job of planting and the soaking wet of the sprout field took its toll.

The days have long since gone when casual labour would come willingly to work in the evenings in the hay and harvest field for nothing more than plenty of bread and boiled bacon and cider. The pattern of life has, of course, changed. Len's son now works the holding. He has a job in cattle transport but farms the Glebe part-time. I can see barley where strawberries grew, a flock of sheep where the late sprouts used to be picked, pigs on free range, a few fowls in the rick-yard. All this is wise management, being less labour intensive. It is good to see continuity on a small farm, the business being handed on grandfather to father, father to son.

I have always recognized Len as a real character, a quiet, unassuming man, handy with horses, his life steeped in the soil. He has left us now, but he is still missed and I can picture him riding his bike home at dusk from the fields with a can of milk from the house cow and a few free-range eggs. Len did use a tractor in his later years but somehow I think he was happier with horses. Weren't we all!

CHAPTER TWENTY-TWO

1939 AND ALL THAT

When a revolution occurs, whether it be industrial or agricultural, it is often not recognized at the time. We look back and say, 'That was a revolution. Things have never been the same after that period of time.'

One such period took place in 1939 at the outbreak of the Second World War. There had been a gradual build-up during the 1930s, as the then Minister of Agriculture, Mr W.S. Morrison, had started schemes for land improvement in the light of the fact that a war looked likely. We paid for farmers' subsidy to dress their pastures with lime and basic slag. Among other such schemes, this application, which farmers took advantage of, improved the pasture and when the land was ploughed up there was improved fertility.

When the War Agricultural Committee was formed farmers were under orders to do what they were told. The ploughing-up campaign turned Britain into essentially an arable country. Farmers who had milking herds were able to retain most of their pasture, others were asked to plough up. 'It wouldn't have done in the Squire's time,' Jim Vale said when the tractors worked on Sundays.

Fordson tractors driven by Land Army girls ploughed land that had never been arable in the lifetime of the older men. These girls from the cities, dressed as if they were at the seaside, produced comments from the staid, corduroyed, hobnailed, Oxford-shirted countrymen. As they bounced on iron seats on their tractors they were to be admired, these factory workers and hairdressers who had come to take the place of men born and bred to the soil. On hot summer days the girls in sun-tops, shorts, and something called a snood on their heads, turned brown in the old meadows.

One old chap said to me, looking at one lass with golden hair, bleached in the sun, ''Tis more than human nature can stand.' They took everything in their stride: fruit picking, harvesting, threshing. Some of the women workers were jealous of this new work-force. 'They will have to do as much as we do,' they told one foreman. No one had ever thought that the city girls could adjust and work on the land.

It was hard for the young farm workers who were not old enough for the Army. They had to compete later with American soldiers at the village hall dances – the boys on low wages in competition for Land Army partners with the smart, brass-ornamented fellows from the States.

The first harvest of corn yielded well on the whole, but wireworm in the old pastures was a problem. They fed on the young shoots of wheat. What a change there was! The smell of ripeness in the fields as harvest drew near was a contrast to the toasting smell of hay. Square Heads Master had been the most common variety of wheat for years, but now we had varieties of a different kind: Jubilee Gem, Wilma, Desprey 80, all bred to yield heavily for the War Effort.

The market gardeners were asked to grow onions for the Army. Many of these men only grew spring onions. The War Agricultural Committee said that they must grow 50 per cent of the onions to harvest as bulb onions. The trade for spring onions was good and the growers in the spring were tempted to pull all the onions green. One man did and was in trouble with the committee.

Apples which had always been sold by variety – the choicest eaters making the most money – were sold by size. The growers had a cardboard measure with holes the size of the apple to be graded. The apples which failed to go through the hole were top quality regardless of variety; the smalls went for cider.

Farmers were ordered to grow potatoes in quantity. They had no equipment for this and had to plough the tubers out of the ground with old-fashioned potato ploughs.

The War Agricultural Committee was a sort of butt in conversation at the village pubs. One chap, it is said, applied for petrol coupons for his tractor. One question on the form said, 'What other means of transport have you got?' The farmer replied, 'One gelding'. The coupons came back to him – six gallons for the tractor and five for the gelding!

There was an influx into the village of folk from outside who bought up farms and holdings but knew very little of how to work the land. One so-called bailiff thought he was planting clover on the hill and lettuce came up instead.

It took all sorts to work the land, and one farmer had been what's known as a 'Dog and Stick' man, making just enough money for him and his wife. His corn was so full of weed that when he threshed it there was more groundsel, chickweed, dock, and thistles than wheat.

In the village the black-out proved to be a problem. One elderly lady only blacked out her windows at the front of her cottage, the Germans would never come to the back she thought. All the time the countryside was changing more than it had in hundreds of years. The young men who went into the Army would never come back to the land. The older men who left the land to work on aerodromes would be pleased with double pay. They would never return to the land. Everywhere machines were taking over.

When animal feed was rationed a pig club was formed in the village, a sort of National Health for pigs. On joining, the pigs were insured against disease, and by forfeiting bacon coupons, which didn't amount to much, rations could be bought for the cottager's pig. Licences were obtained to kill the pig on the day when the butcher could come. Len, who worked for me, said one morning, 'I shall have to go to the Food Office. I've a licence to kill my sow pig and she is in use.' This meant she was on heat. The old idea was that if a pig is killed while on heat the bacon won't cure properly. Len was not taking that risk.

'At the Food Office,' Len went on, 'what do you think? A woman came to the desk. I said, I want to see a man. What I have got to tell you un't for women's ears.'

The office obliged Len and he told his story.

Things were changing fast among the middle-class, middle-aged ladies of the village. They had always gone to have their perms at Greens, the 'Up Market' hairdresser in the town. But 'Sorry, we can't make appointments,' was the answer to lots of phone calls. The BBC had come to Wood Norton and the ladies from there were keeping Greens busy with their fancy hair-dos. What a shock.

The evacuees from Birmingham brought with them a sort of added interest in home life. They came at seven or eight years old, quite ignorant of country life, but how well they adapted to the black-out, and the lack of cinema and fish and chip shop.

'What you bin doing today, Uncle?' one eight-year-old girl asked me. It was November and we were harvesting the mangolds.

'I've been pulling mangolds,' I said.

She gave me a funny look, replying, 'Yow don't pull mangles, yow turns 'um.'

These evacuees mixed with the village children and the dialect, which had been rural Worcestershire and Gloucestershire, became a mixture of city and country, the Birmingham influence.

As the city folk came from London, Birmingham and Bristol the Women's Institute doubled in numbers. The new farming overseers from the War Agricultural Committee, college-trained, spoke differently from the local men of the land. The pubs were changing, the incomers drank shorts and ate scampi and chips; cider was frowned upon and called Agricultural Brandy.

The threat of invasion was real and the native villagers got used to being organized by the Food Ministry. The War Agricultural Committee and those that didn't join the Home Guard were in the Civil Defence.

1939 AND ALL THAT

Cecil Day Lewis wrote in 1940:

Among the stubble a farmer and I keep watch
For whatever may come to injure our countryside —
Light-signals, parachutes, bombs, or sea invaders.
The moon looks over the hill's shoulders, and hope
Mans the old ramparts of an English night.

All over the countryside
Moon dazed men are peering out for invaders.

The Home Guard, in the first instance known as the LDV (Local Defence Volunteers), were under a colonel who fought in the Boer War. They were armed with 12-bore shotguns when they did their guard duty on Bredon Hill. A wooden hut erected by the Cuckoo Pen, a vantage point looking over the vale, was where two men took guard duty at dawn and dusk. The colonel, one of the old school of officers, recruited a team of men who could be described as The Awkward Squad, a mixture of 'hobbledehoys' and ex-service chaps from the First World War. He said to one cowman, 'I haven't seen you amongst my men, Stones. Are you going to join?'

Stones, a 'dry bread wet' sort of chap, replied, 'I might have a walk up the Hill one night.'

'That's not the spirit, man,' came the reply from the old Brass Hat.

Bill, who worked as porter-in-charge at the railway station, told me his story of guarding the hill. In those days the hill was alive with rabbits. Bill took the opportunity to supplement his meagre meat ration with rabbit meat. Some nights he shot six rabbits; one night he killed twelve.

One footpath to the Cuckoo Pen went through an orchard. Jim, a corporal, took life very seriously and could be described as exacting. He was a little early one evening at dusk. He waited for

157

his partner, Len, by the stile. As Len approached Jim shouted, 'Halt. Who goes there?' There was no reply so Jim levelled his rifle at Len and called, 'Halt or I fire.' The answer came back, 'Don't be so damned silly. Yer know who I be.'

On parade one Sunday morning my tractor driver, who had just joined the Guard, told me of a chap named Hooper who was among the volunteers having a rifle inspection. Inside Hooper's rifle the officer found a spider. 'Are you breeding livestock, Hooper?' he shouted.

The lieutenant told his men that in the event of an invasion he would ring the church bells. 'Nobody must ring the bells but me,' he added. 'Even if King Dick tells you to ring the bells, you must not ring them.'

George had been at school with the lieutenant and the two had grown up together as market gardeners. He couldn't bring himself to call his old school friend Lieutenant, or even Sir, and said, 'Whoever is King Dick then Bob?'

It was mid-summer, the days were long and the weather was hot. Orders were issued to the men that military manoeuvres were to take place on Bredon Hill the following Saturday. GHQ was a local pub, and the officers, who met regularly there, had a petrol allowance and they were quite entitled to their pub visits despite the efforts of the local policeman to summons them.

The men assembled at La Lu Farm at midday on Saturday and they were organized in two units. The object was for one unit to take possession of the tower, Parson's Folly, while the other men were to prevent them. The defenders of the tower won the war game and took prisoners, and that night was to be spent in La Lu barn. The lieutenant told his men that they would be on iron rations but that there would still be plenty to eat. A pot of soup was boiled over an open fire in the barn and each man was issued with a hard biscuit.

'Is that all we are having, Bob?' said his old school friend.

'That's it, the Colonel's orders,' was the reply.

As darkness fell the men in the Home Guard had gone hungry to bed in the hay of La Lu barn. Private Brown knew Bredon Hill like the back of his hand. At midnight he led some of his pals down the hill into Pig Lane to the Apple Tree pub. He knew the landlord, who got up and gave the men a pint of beer each and some bread and cheese. They then found their way to their houses and slept with their wives, returning to the hill early the next morning. The officer spent the night in a cottage near the barn and never knew the men had deserted.

Arthur, an ex-Grenadier from the First World War and a corporal in the Home Guard, lay on the hay beside Wilson. Arthur was a carter off the land who could plough a straight furrow, but to march was more than could be expected and he walked with a kind of nautical roll. Wilson had his dreams – they may have been of fairy princesses or bathing belles, who knows? He snored the night away beside Arthur, who got no sleep at all. Then Wilson slipped one arm around Arthur's waist and then the other. When a bristly face met his, Arthur could stand it no longer. Waking his companion up he shouted, 'Ay, Wils. It yunt Alice you be making up to, it's me.'

Wilson, waking up and finding himself in a hay barn partly filled with men, sighed and whispered, 'Damn it. I thought I was sleeping anant Alice and her wanting me. Still, perhaps tomorrow night.'

These exercises on the hill would have been useful had the enemy landed. Who knows, our little mob might have used their initiative and scattered the enemy. They would have done their best I'm sure. One thing is certain, these men of the land, market gardeners and stockmen, were good shots with their 12-bore guns. To witness Cousin Tom, a market gardener, knock over a running rabbit was worth seeing. I'd rather have been on his side when it came to a shooting match!

Wilson's psychology had a different bent. A man who had hardly ever been out of the village when his employer converted the wheels of the muck carts to pneumatic tyres, Wilson failed to keep them pumped up.

'That tyre's a bit flat, Wils,' the boss said one morning.

'Ay. 'Tis I s'pose, but it's only at the bottom where it touches the ground.'

He used some unusual expressions to describe nature. When the crows were at what is known as 'breaknecks' Wilson said, 'They be cider making up there.' It was a sign of rain.

As a boy, Wilson drove the horses and wagons from the hay field to the rick-yard. One day he said to the men in the field, 'Mind what you be saying down yer. The gaffer's got his field glasses in the rick-yard and he 'ull hear every word.'

We of the Civil Defence were a mixed lot; some of us were market gardeners, there was a small pig, sheep and poultry farmer, and a young tractor driver. Sammy, the deputy warden, a sheep and pig farmer, was a very inquisitive sort of chap. He was a Jew and some village folk benefited when he sold his bacon coupons. One night when the planes were overhead on their way to Coventry, Sammy said to me, 'Mr Hill's black-out was not very good last night. I will go and check it.'

We stood in the road as Sammy went up the footpath and knelt down under Mr Hill's window peeping through.

'What do you think you are doing down there, you Peeping Tom?'

'It's your black-out. It wasn't very good last night. I'm checking.'

Mr Hill replied, 'Get off down my path before I put the toe of my shoe into your ass.'

We tittered at old Sammy as he came down into the road saying, 'This job is not very pleasant at times.'

The WI turned out at the village hall when the siren sounded and made tea in case of casualties. The problem was, they switched the lights on before putting the black-out up and the bottom of the village was lit up like Crystal Palace. The planes were passing over en route to Birmingham and Coventry.

Tom Hunting with his mother and father

I was issued with a canvas tank to hold water, canvas buckets and hoses, together with a pump, as a mini fire brigade. No incendiaries bothered us, just a chimney fire, which we dealt with, in a thatched cottage.

One warden, having been up without much sleep for three nights running, had heard Churchill on the radio, stressing the importance of keeping up our morale. Over a pint in the pub this chap declared, 'It's all very well for Churchill talking about our morals. If I get another night without sleep all my morals will be gone.'

A couple came from the city, the man to work on a neighbouring farm to avoid the Army. His wife was a school teacher, and they lived in a farmhouse opposite mine. A screaming bomb came over one night and this chap described how he jumped on top of his wife in their bed to protect her in case the roof fell in. The locals in the pub were quite amused. That night a bomb cleaned out a duck pond in a neighbouring village, and four unexploded bombs fell in one of my fields known as The Needlelands. A neighbour called that morning asking me if I'd been cleaning the brook out as he saw heaps of clay. The Army exploded the bombs, but what a lot of work we had filling in the craters.

Sammy entertained us those winter nights when we drank coffee with J.B., our head warden, who had made a shelter in the garden. Sammy insisted that our village was not worth a bomb. His health failed towards the end of the war and he went to hospital. When I visited him, this little man of ninety, he always wanted to know how much my lambs made at market. A farmer at heart, who always kept a few sheep in his orchard, he dreamed of sheep and called them from his hospital bed, waking the ward. So Sammy finished his days in a private ward.

In all the Home Guard and the Civil Defence in a West Midlands village was much the same as depicted in 'Dad's Army' on the television. A truly amateur set-up, but if tested, they would have done their best in an emergency.

But 1939 was a watershed when life in the village changed, never to be the same again. I wonder, had it not been for the war, whether wheat and barley would have grown on those acres which had been neglected for so long. Would the boar thistles still have grown, tree-like on Bredon Hill? And would we import all our grain from Canada?

Would the sons of the little master men who had tilled the small holdings of Ayles Acre or Hell's Acre, have followed their fathers, growing fruit and vegetables instead of buying cars and motor bikes which took them to the factories of nearby towns?

Before 1939 it was rare for anyone to come to live in the village or for anyone to leave. If a furniture van came the children followed it and watched the unloading, and were so pleased if children from away came to the village school. Most boys leaving school went to work on the land. There was a spirit in the fields at bait time which is long since gone.

Local football was supported by local folk. It would have been treachery to support teams of the first division, such as Manchester United. Maybe there was loyalty and rivalry between villages.

So the old rural culture slowly disappeared and alien voices were heard in the village. Some who came thought of us as swede-gnawers. They had high-falutin ideas for street lighting, social centres, dramatic societies, which didn't always work. The families with cars went shopping and to the theatre in Cheltenham, and the insular life of the village was gone for ever.